THE AMERICA'S CUP 1987
THE OFFICIAL RECORD

THE AMERICA'S CUP 1987
THE OFFICIAL RECORD

THE AMERICA'S CUP 1987
THE OFFICIAL RECORD

Bob Fisher and Bob Ross
Introduction by John Bertrand

Published with the cooperation of
The Royal Perth Yacht Club

Henry Holt and Company
New York

Published in the United States by
Henry Holt and Company, Inc., 521 Fifth Avenue,
New York, New York 10175.

Distributed in Canada by Fitzhenry & Whiteside Limited,
195 Allstate Parkway, Markham, Ontario L3R 4T8.

Library of Congress Catalog Card Number: 87-45224

The publishers would like to extend special thanks to
IBM Australia and Fuji Hanimex for their cooperation on
this book.

Typesetting by Christype, Australia
Color reproduction by Multicolor, Australia
Designed by Neil H. Clitheroe

ISBN 0-8050-0580-3

First American Edition

Printed in Hong Kong by Imago/Lee Fung Asco

10 9 8 7 6 5 4 3 2 1

CONTENTS

ACKNOWLEDGEMENTS

The Royal Perth Yacht Club

The Royal Perth Yacht Club

After they had swept up the champagne corks and dispersed the euphoria on 27th September 1983, the 2,000 members of the Royal Perth Yacht Club looked at one another and realised that Alan Bond, with *Australia II's* win of the previous day, had handed them not only the America's Cup but the enormous responsibilities of becoming its trustee, finding a defender and conducting the 26th Defence of the America's Cup.

The Royal Perth YC, formed on 13th November 1865, housed deep tradition within its pleasant clubhouse nestled inside Pelican Point on the Swan River. It had organised many successful championships for international keelboat and dinghy classes, but could this club at the opposite side of the world from the New York Yacht Club, without a presence on the open water off Fremantle, where the event would be sailed, conduct an America's Cup? Fortunately, among the club's yachtsmen and race officers were some visionaries with entrepreneurial skills who quickly realised that freeing the Cup from its 126 years' sanctuary within the West 44th Street Manhattan clubhouse of the New York Yacht Club would escalate the stature of the event beyond its yacht racing pinnacle to make it one of the world's biggest international sporting occasions.

With yacht racing at all levels steadily embracing commercial sponsorships and America's Cup campaign budgets at A$ 20 millions or more demanding them, the club found itself standing at a new corner, balancing the Corinthian stature of the event, so carefully preserved by the New York Yacht Club, and the professional approach needed if it were to survive.

It correctly perceived the scale of the America's Cup 1987 from a long way back, budgeted for it and set about finding the sponsorship help it needed to ensure the event would bring credit to the club, and to Australia, without becoming a financial burden on its members, many of whom were to contribute substantially as volunteer helpers.

The Royal Perth Yacht Club Commodore, Alan Crewe, at the official launch of Kookaburra III.

Previous page: The Royal Perth Yacht Club headquarters in Crawley Bay.

First step was the formation of the America's Cup committee in January, 1984. Dr. Stan Reid took on the onerous and time-consuming task of being its Chairman with the proviso that the club gave the committee autonomy and gave him permission to select his own committee men. Each of the ten this astute and steady administrator chose was given a substantial responsibility and stuck to it. After more than a hundred meetings before the Cup, the team had not changed. The committee's only full-time professionals were Noel Robins, an internationally experienced and successful sailor who skippered Australia in the 1977 America's Cup challenge, and four secretarial assistants.

Through its marketing body, ADAC Ltd., the club gained the support of initial major sponsors — Australian Airlines; BP Australia; BHP; Coca-Cola; General Motors Holden; Macquarie Network; Swan Brewery Co. Ltd.; and Westpac — towards meeting its original budget of A$3 million. Before the Cup, that was to rise to A$6 million and more sponsors were enlisted, prominent amongst them White Horse Whisky.

On Challenger Harbour, constructed next to Fremantle's Fishing Boat Harbour by the West Australian Government at a cost of A$8.25 million to provide berths for the defender and challenger syndicates, Royal Perth established a marina for its official vessels, a measurement pen for the 12-Metres and its neat and practical brick annexe clubhouse that will serve as a useful base for regattas well into the future.

The club contributed through sponsorships from IBM, Hanimex-Fuji and Seiko a half share, with the Commonwealth and West Australian Governments providing the other half, of the A$1.5 million spent on transforming a disused indoor hockey stadium into the most modern, best equipped media centre any of the veteran yachting writers had ever seen, to satisfy the intense international interest in the event. More than 3,000 people from 25 countries were eventually accredited. Managed by veteran wire-service journalist Lyall Rowe, it was open 24 hours a day, had 200 working spaces, all the electronic tools needed to write, transmit or broadcast, and provided a flood of information.

Challenger Harbour, under construction in September 1985.

Answering criticism, notably from Alan Bond, that the club had spent too much on the facilities and hampered the chances of the defence syndicates by competing with them for the sponsorship money, Noel Robins said: 'Right from the start, it was agreed Royal Perth Yacht Club would run the event and the syndicates would run the boats.'

The success of this longest and most intense regatta the world had even seen depended heavily on volunteer helpers. The Royal Perth Yacht Club had 300 rostered to help run the racing and the media centre. On race days, up to 120 of them would be on the water. The racing was well run with consistently high standard committee work that would not have been easy in the usually punishing wave-pattern of Gage Roads.

The Royal Perth Yacht Club excelled, too, on the fun side of the regatta. Not only competitors and the club members, but the whole of Perth, it seemed, wanted to become involved. An old wool store was transformed into a bushland setting so that 2,500 people could dance at the America's Cup Ball. Much earlier in the regatta the club hosted an even bigger bash — a cocktail party for 3,500 on the lawns of the Pelican Point clubhouse, with the star of the evening the 'Auld Mug' itself rising, as a Holy Grail should, out of swirling mist from the shoreside barge. For all of the visitors: thanks, Royal Perth Yacht Club, you did it well. And, in West Australian fashion, you did it grandly.

INTRODUCTION

By John Bertrand

Dennis Conner's Stars & Stripes team won the America's Cup, off Fremantle, with a swift 4-0 despatch of the Australian defender *Kookaburra III*, because of a significant boat speed advantage – perhaps the largest we have seen in the past twenty years of Cup racing. Conner's Sail America syndicate was well organised, particularly in its ability to bring together streams of research and the talents of its three designers – Britton Chance Jr, Bruce Nelson and Dave Pedrick – and to transfer the technology to yacht racing excellence.

A major coup was to appoint John Marshall as design coordinator. It is very difficult, in any country, to find people with Marshall's technical, sail-making and organisational qualifications and his ability to draw the various resources together. His skills meant that the syndicate was able to make steady, positive improvement as the summer rolled on. *Stars & Stripes* was not 'sandbagging', concealing her true form, in the early round robin series of the Louis Vuitton Cup. She was trying to win races early but was off pace.

In the America's Cup campaigning, yachts are so refined in their tuning that most go forward one step, back two and then forward one again. But *Stars & Stripes* was able to make steady progress.

The design team had a very good grasp of the technology; their ability to transfer theory to practice and the step-by-step changes they made to the boat in Fremantle generally always resulted in improvement. By the time the challenger final came, the boat was a formidable weapon, able upwind either to point higher or foot off faster for speed than an opponent and downwind to have at least equal speed and against *Kookaburra III* often to be faster.

The syndicate's designers and their research assistants took some risks in November and December but they had a calculated grasp on the changes they made to their boat. And Dennis and his crew, gathering tremendous confidence as their boat improved, sailed very, very well.

On the defender's side *Australia IV*, the product of thirteen years of America's Cup experience, fell a little below the requirements for a successful defender. It is always hard for a winning team to set the fresh levels of excellence that have to be established every time a new contest begins. I feel

Previous page: Excited well-wishers jammed Stars & Stripes' *docks, by land and sea.*

16

the syndicate suffered through the lack of Alan Bond's direct involvement in the early stages of the campaign compared to the build-up to the 1983 America's Cup when he made some important decisions.

So the defence went to the Taskforce syndicate. They made a superb effort, developing boats, sails and crews, but it was very unlikely that a rookie syndicate would win the America's Cup. The Bond syndicate, with thirteen years under the belt, was the obvious one to defend. You can't practise the America's Cup. You can practise everything else over the three-year lead up but you cannot practise the eleventh hour encounter.

In the eleventh hour, with more poise and confidence, *Kookaburra III* could have won the first race, a very tough one. But that would not have changed the outcome of the regatta. The basic proportions of *Kookaburra III* were not as good as those of *Stars & Stripes*. From knowledge gathered progressively from *Stars & Stripes '83*, a small boat; *Stars & Stripes '85*, a big boat; and *Stars & Stripes '86*, a radical boat, the designers were able to produce in *Stars & Stripes '87* a bigger and heavier boat which was unbeatable in 16 knots of wind and over but still able to win races in a wind of 10-12 knots.

The America's Cup season in Fremantle will be etched for ever on the memories of all those privileged to be there: the great regatta organisation from Royal Perth Yacht Club, the hospitality of the people of the wonderfully refurbished, beautiful port city, the cameraderie of the competitors, the magnitude and quality of the spectacle of racing conducted in fresh winds under clear blue skies on clear blue water.

If the Cup is next sailed in a place like Hawaii where there are strong winds, blue skies and therefore the guarantee of good television pictures, as we had in Fremantle, it will move into a new dimension of sophistication, meeting the forecast of A$50 million syndicate budgets. If however the Cup is sailed in an area of low winds, the corporate investment needed to sustain budgets of that magnitude will not be realised and the event will go backwards in terms of commercial viability.

Generous Aussie graffito applauds the champion in its own way.

Conner the mean; Conner the moody; Conner the magnificent.

Given the type of television coverage generated from Fremantle, and the sponsorship support made possible by the liberalisation of the international yacht racing Rule 26 which has restricted display of sponsor advertising, the Cup will move towards the international appeal of Formula 1 motor racing.

The technology will come from various sources around the world much more freely than before and expert crews will be recruited from many countries, given national status for the event. As an extreme example, you could see Americans and Germans crewing boats built by Saudi Arabian money flying the British flag. That degree of commercialisation would only be realised at America's Cup level, where corporate involvement has any relevance; it would not diminish the appeal of mainstream, amateur yachting, but would create something to which the young could aspire.

To win back the Cup, Australians must do some lateral thinking: scour the world, not only to draw in the technology but to find the people to adminster and race the yachts. Although we do now have a 12-Metre experience base, Australia is not big enough to go it alone. We must take a leap-frog step on the road ahead – bite off another twenty years of progress in the standards we set ourselves. From the technology point of view, 12-Metre design has only scratched the surface of available knowledge from the aircraft industry and from shipbuilding hydrodynamics.

After thirteen years of being involved with winning the America's Cup, I was disappointed to see the trophy that took so long to win lost so quickly. Next time round, I will help on a larger scale than I was able to do this time.

Although the Australian people showed tremendous sportsmanship in acknowledging the defeat, I felt they lacked a sense of history of the event. They did not comprehend how hard it would be to win back the Cup.

To win it back will require an even greater sense of commitment and dedication than Dennis and his syndicate demonstrated this time. I fully expect to see that in the next challenge, because I have a lot of faith in the Australian fighting spirit.   John Bertrand

CHAPTER ONE

And Then There Were Two...

And Then There Were Two...

The yachting gypsies jetted into Perth steadily through August and the early September of 1986, set up their camps in welcoming Fremantle and spread their colourful sails like cloaks across the clean blue carpet of water known as Gage Roads, venue for the greatest yachting regatta the world has ever seen, to culminate in the 26th Defence of the America's Cup.

Most of them had met before at regattas around the world – the Olympics, Admiral's Cup, SORC, the international match racing circuit and world championships; but never before in its 135 years' history had the America's Cup attracted such a collection of fine sailing talent.

Some, like the New York Yacht Club, had begun to set up their caravans – docks, engineering shops and sail lofts; on Fremantle's Fishing Boat Harbour soon after the Cup changed hands in 1983, alongside the defenders. Others, through financial constraints, arrived only just in time for the event; and one, headed by the man who lost the Cup, Dennis Conner, was a late arrival for another reason. In the steady trade winds of Hawaii, he believed he had found the ideal conditions to test full size, with a collection of five boats, the design ideas needed to win in the 12-30 knot winds expected off Fremantle during the period of the Cup regatta.

On 5th October the seagoing gypsies began their racing; on 4th February, after 324 races, Conner's *Stars & Stripes,* with a definite upwind speed edge and immaculately handled by an experienced crew, gained her fourth straight win over Iain Murray's *Kookaburra III,* equally well handled by a fine young crew, to win the America's Cup. In between the regatta held all the twists and turns of a fine murder-mystery novel, with each page stamped by the characters as one by one they were despatched.

First to go was *Courageous.* Designed 13 years earlier by Olin Stephens, she twice successfully defended the Cup, against the Australian challenges of 1974 and 1977, and campaigned in the 1980 and 1983 defence trials. Leonard

Previous page: A mastless Stars & Stripes *arrives at Fishing Boat Harbour, Fremantle, a scene initially dominated by the Bond syndicate dock at left.*

Royal Perth Yacht Club Commodore, Alan Crewe, receiving the America's Cup Deed of Gift from the New York Yacht Club Commodore, Arthur Santry.

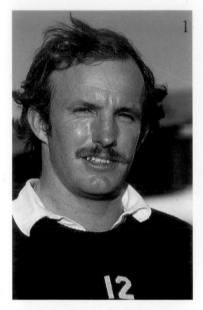 1

2

3

 4

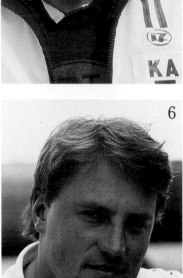

 5

6

THE SKIPPERS

Defenders

AMERICA'S CUP DEFENCE 1987 LIMITED
1. Colin Beashel *Australia IV*
2. Gordon Lucas *Australia III*

EASTERN AUSTRALIAN DEFENCE SYNDICATE
3. Fred Neill *Steak 'n' Kidney*
4. Phil Thompson *Steak 'n' Kidney*

SOUTH AUSTRALIA CHALLENGE
5. John Savage *South Australia*

TASKFORCE '87 LIMITED
6. Iain Murray *Kookaburra III*
7. Peter Gilmour *Kookaburra II*

Challengers

HEART OF AMERICA CHALLENGE
8. Buddy Melges *Heart of America*

US MERCHANT MARINE ACADEMY FOUNDATION
9. John Kolius *America II*

EAGLE FOUNDATION
10. Rod Davis *Eagle*

 7

 8

 9

 10

 11

 12

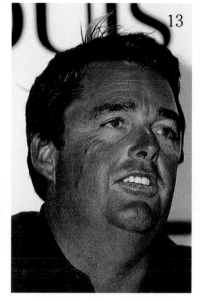 13

 14

 15

NEW ZEALAND CHALLENGE
11. Chris Dickson *New Zealand*

BRITISH AMERICA'S CUP CHALLENGE PLC
12. Harold Cudmore *White Crusader*

SAIL AMERICA FOUNDATION FOR INTERNATIONAL UNDERSTANDING
13. Dennis Conner *Stars & Stripes*

GOLDEN GATE FOUNDATION
14. Tom Blackaller *USA*

SECRET COVE/TRUE NORTH
15. Terry Neilson *Canada II*

CHALLENGE KIS FRANCE
16. Marc Pajot *French Kiss*

MARSEILLES SYNDICATE
17. Yves Pajot *Challenge France*

AZZURRA SYNDICATE
18. Mauro Pelaschier *Azzurra*

CONSORZIO ITALIA
19. Aldo Migliaccio *Italia*

COURAGEOUS CHALLENGE
20. David Vietor *Courageous IV*

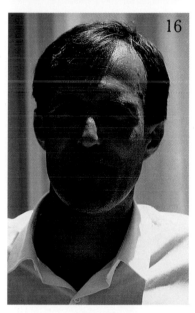 16

 17

 18

 19

 20

Greene, an inventor in the aircraft industry, tried to breathe new life into her old body with a radical keel shape and trim-tab system and entered her as *Courageous IV*.

Operating as the last of the amateurs in a totally professional field, Greene's challenge was through the Yale Corinthian Yacht Club, but the boat, as well as that notion, was out of date. *Courageous* was beaten by margins of up to eleven and a half minutes, won only one race, against *Challenge France*, broke two booms and the hearts of Greene and his amiable skipper Dave Vietor, who once owned the boat. She was retired from the competition at the end of the first round robin.

Challenge France was the next to go. Funding to campaign the yacht in Australia came too late for this unusual looking design by Daniel Andrieu to reach her potential. She arrived only just in time for the regatta and won two races in the first round robin, over *Azzurra* after the Italian yacht retired with steering failure, and *French Kiss* with a win in the protest room for a pre-start infringement after *French Kiss* had crossed the finish line 17:40 ahead. Yves Pajot, brother of *French Kiss* skipper Marc Pajot, and the more subdued of the two, skippered *Challenge France*. She won no more races and, after breaking her mast on day six of the third round robin, retired from the regatta half way through that round.

The end of the third round robin in the Louis Vuitton Cup was the end too of *Canada II*, *Heart of America*, *Azzurra*, *Italia*, *White Crusader* and, in the first major twist of the plot in this mystery novel, *America II*. The New York Yacht Club's challenger, with its US$15 million budget and very thorough preparation, was high on everybody's list of favourites. The programme involved three new Twelves designed by Bill Langan of Sparkman & Stephens, the most impressive of all the shore facilities put together by Cap'n Tuna, more correctly Arthur J. Wullschleger, as operations director, strong management under Vice Chairman William B. Packer, and a great looking crew headed by the cool Texan John Kolius who, sailing *Courageous*, fully extended Conner's

Bloodied but unbowed, Courageous *at her fifth attempt for the Cup could do little more than provide an insight to the racing for the new America's Cup sailors.*

Opening of the defender series. Left to right: John Savage, Warren Jones, Ken Court, Peter Gilmour, Iain Murray, Graham Spurling and Syd Fischer.

One hundred and thirty four ounces of stirling silver crafted by Garrards in 1848 as a wine ewer and mutilated by the members of the New York Yacht Club, who pierced its bottom in order that a retaining bolt might be fitted. Originally the silver cup, presented to the schooner America for winning a Royal Yacht Squadron race around the Isle of Wight, would have been used to serve any type of wine, including champagne, to guests in dinner at the houses of English gentry. This particular one has become the symbol of world yachting supremacy: the America's Cup.

Liberty in the 1983 defender eliminations.

America II's demise came on the second last day of racing when, after defeat at the hands of *New Zealand 7,* it became mathematically impossible for her to go into the semi-finals. Under the burden of a moment in history – the end of the New York Yacht Club's 135 year unbroken association with the Cup – the laconic Kolius bared his soul to the press conference inquisition: 'You have got to realise the New York Yacht Club is not just an entity that is rolling along and it's some big ogre or something. There are a lot of people with a lot of hopes and dreams that came to an end today. Being tagged as this entity that you guys like to refer to as the New York Yacht Club, well, I've got news for you. There's a bunch of people that shed a lot of tears down at the dock tonight and they put in a lot of effort for a long time and pretty much gave it their best shot.'

The British challenge was late getting under way, but it brought a new thrust of commercialism that sat strangely under the burgee of the challenging, venerable and conservative Royal Thames Yacht Club. The syndicate, headed by Graham Walker, was a publicly listed commercial company engaged in yacht racing promotion. It put together a £4.8 million budget to support a campaign that was lean, but effective compared with those of the 'gorilla' syndicates – helmsman Chris Law's unique way of describing the big spenders of the Cup summer.

It built two boats: the first a conventional development 12-Metre from Ian Howlett, designer of *Lionheart* and *Victory '83;* the second a very radical design from David Hollom, known to the crew as 'Hippo' because of the way her above water shape bulbed out over a very fine underbody. The British arrived in Fremantle in April and trained throughout the winter, but there was not enough time to develop the second boat. Skipper Harold Cudmore and his crew were quite happy with the original *Crusader,* which became *White Crusader* after White Horse Whisky invested £1.1 million in the syndicate in September 1986. The syndicate pushed Rule 26, which restricts sponsorshop

They said 'You can take a White Horse anywhere' and the English were prepared to try.

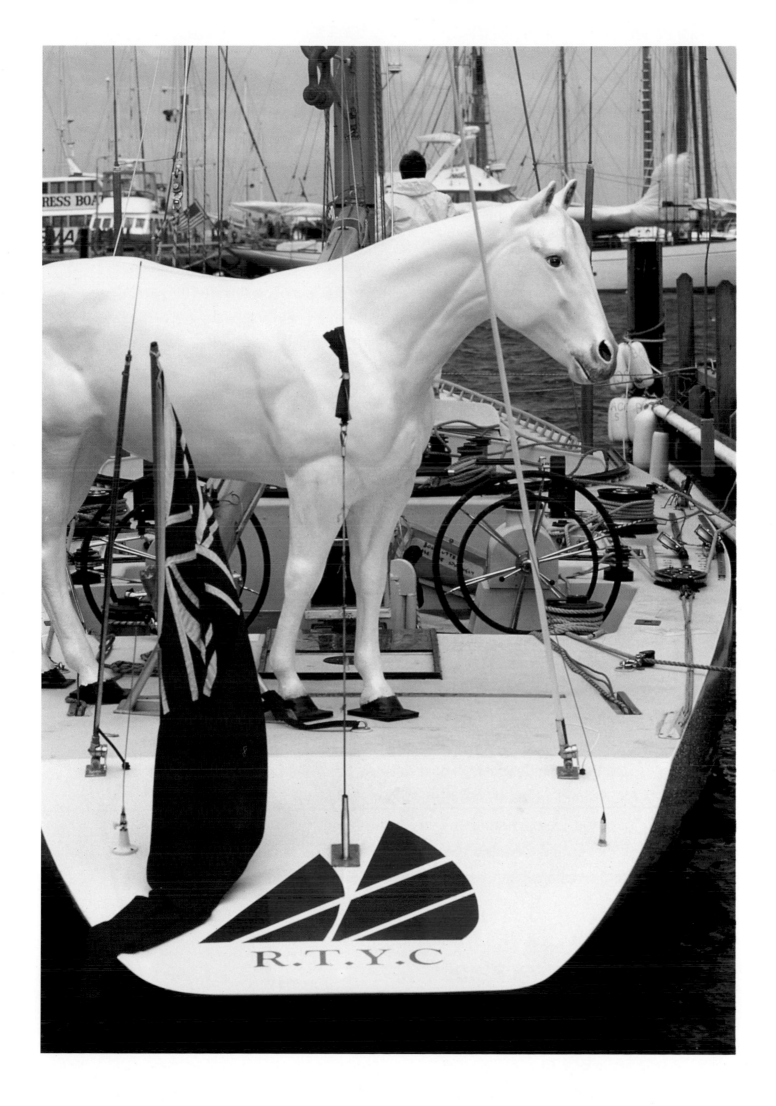

and advertising on the hull and sails, to its limits in order to gain mileage for its sponsor.

White Crusader was extremely well sailed with Cudmore, established as one of the world's best match racers, taking the starts and then handing over the wheel to Chris Law, so that he could concentrate on tactics. Another first class helmsman, Eddie Warden-Owen, was in the afterguard as navigator. Tactically, they were one of the best and most aggressive. Although the British team worked hard on improving her, *White Crusader* was a shade off the pace, especially on the runs. The curly headed Cudmore said before the start of the last round robin: 'This is where you have to perform; perform or go home. Isn't that it?' It was.

The two Italian syndicates rolled into Fremantle with the best crew clothing, motor cycles and scooters and each with two new boats backed by big budgets. They remained bankrupt in boat speed. Each had to discard their more radical yacht after testing against the predecessors off Fremantle showed them to be slower or too erratic in performance. Mauro Pellaschier emerged from a bewildering change of principals in the last months before the regatta to again skipper *Azzurra,* the one designed by Andrea Vallicelli.

Aldo Migliaccio skippered *Italia* – until the third round robin that is, when broken ribs, suffered in an accident with his Alfa Romeo, kept him ashore. *Italia* was designed by Giorgetti & Magrini after a consultancy with Ian Howlett. She was well steered by Tommaso Chieffi, sailed some good races, but had difficulty when the typically short, sharp wave pattern of Gage Roads kicked up.

Canada II, a re-model of the 1983 challenger designed by Bruce Kirby, came to Fremantle with high hopes after good showings against US challengers *Heart of America* and *USA* during training and informal racing in California. Finn and Laser champion Terry Neilson led a mostly young crew with sailmaker and Olympic medallist Hans Fogh as mainsheet trimmer and alternative helmsman, providing most of the experience and a lot of skill. The

Dressed by Gucci, the Italians were readily assimilated by the huge expatriate contingent that dominates Fremantle's harbours.

CANADA II, *the Bruce Kirby design, started life as* CANADA I *but a new bow and a new stern were fitted for 1987.*

Right: There is no substitute for hard work when preparing the underwater surfaces of a 12-Metre; Eagle *gets the treatment.*

Canadians, however, had tactical problems. Andy Roy was replaced as tactician by Greg Tawaststjerna after the first round robin. After some good early races the Canadians appeared to lose confidence in their boat and themselves.

Eagle, designed by Johan Valentijn and skippered by match racing expert Rod Davis, challenged from Newport Harbor Yacht Club in California. Delays in fund raising and the design programme, in which Valentijn ran through a number of far-out concepts, led to a late launching. In Fremantle, she struggled for pace from the start of the first round robin and there were internal difficulties. America's Cup veteran Gerry Driscoll resigned as general manager of the syndicate before the start of the second round robin 'due to philosophical differences'.

Before the third round robin, *Eagle* had a drastic keel change. After two weeks in Steve Ward's boat shed, she emerged with a curved down surfboard shape at the bottom of the keel root instead of the thick wings she had carried in the earlier racing. *Eagle* appeared to be no faster and won only against *Azzurra* and *Challenge France*.

A yacht which did improve dramatically from a keel wing modification between the second and third rounds robin was *Heart of America*, skippered by the fabled Mid-West sailor and raconteur Buddy Melges. She was designed by a team which included Jim Gretzky, Scott Graham, Duncan MacLane and Eric Schlageter. They added about three feet to the width of the tips on the winglets. After winning his first race in the third round robin, over *America II*, Melges said: 'The bow instead of chopping here and chopping over there, all of a sudden started to sort of screw itself through the water, with the winglets and tiplets and all that. The tiplets are further aft and when the boat heels a little bit it picks up that lateral resistance which seems to be further aft and it starts to balance as well.'

Melges, in praising his tactician David Dellenbaugh, said he was unlike his previous tactician, Gary Jobson, who resigned from the boat to concentrate on television commitments during the Cup. 'Gary and I in the same boat, we got a little hyped and all of a sudden, we've got to get those Valiums aboard. But with Dave you wonder if he's on them, he's so cool. And I haven't been excited at all. Even today, when we went out against John Kolius and *America II,* I am looking for stimuli. I tripped twice in the back of the boat, hit my head and then I got mad and I was alright.'

Heart of America did not make the semi-finals, but Melges was snapped up as a commentator, by Channel 7, to continue amusing and mystifying Australian television viewers of the Cup regatta.

Over on the defenders' course, *South Australia* dropped out after four races of the third round robin. The Ben Lexcen update of *Australia II,* like her Bond syndicate sister *Australia III,* which was retired after the second round robin, was just outclassed by the newer generation yachts developed for the Fremantle conditions, like the *Kookaburras* and *Australia IV.*

The South Australian syndicate initiated by Adelaide advertising executive Roger Lloyd to boost the state in its 150th birthday celebrations during 1986, was backed by 150 sponsoring companies and greatly helped by a A$1 million subsidy from the Australian government. With Sir James Hardy, helmsman of *Gretel II* in the 1970 challenge, *Southern Cross* in 1974 and *Australia* in 1980 as sailing director, the syndicate campaigned initially with the Bond syndicate.

South Australia was fast in light winds and smooth seas but, despite many changes to keel, displacement, rig and sails, she could never handle the typically windy, choppy conditions of Gage Roads, although she was well sailed with Phil Thompson steering and John Savage, who skippered *Challenge 12* in the 1983 eliminations, as skipper and tactician.

She had an eventful regatta; bowman Andy Dyer went overboard with the spinnaker while preparing the sail for hoisting and was tangled in it under the boat until crewmen dragged him aboard three minutes later. Seventeen days after that Dyer and sewerman Peter Wall-Smith were washed overboard

Overleaf: 'It's nice up here but I've had enough.' Bowman on South Australia.

on the first reach whilst securing the dropped headsail and, through a communications mix up, were in the water for a quarter of an hour before being picked up by a chase boat. Helmsman Phil Thompson was hurled overboard by the impact when *Steak 'n' Kidney* and *South Australia* collided heavily and was lucky not to have been crushed between the two yachts. He was in the water for ten minutes before being rescued; both yachts were holed, with *South Australia* suffering a two foot long gash in her topsides and *Steak 'n' Kidney* splitting her bow; both were disqualified.

South Australia was sold to two Swedish yachtsmen before the end of the second round robin; she buckled her mast before the start on the fifth day of the third series and was withdrawn.

The challenger semi-finals cleanly and swiftly ended the hopes of *French Kiss* and *USA*. Marc Pajot and his young team brought a completely fresh French approach to the America's Cup and they were fast right out of the box, impressing all with their two wins and general showing in the 12-Metre World Championship. They pushed Rule 26 almost beyond its limit with the name – Kis France, parent of the international fast film processing and key cutting group, was the principal sponsor. She had an innovative design by Philippe Briand which was shaped entirely in a computer and Briand was helped in the analysis by engineers at the French Space Research Centre (CNES) and aircraft manufacturer Dassault. It featured rounded hull sections with large girth measurements that made *French Kiss* look in some ways like Briand's ocean racing designs and had a swept back keel with wings instead of the *Australia II* upside down shape, which had been the starting point for most of the other Twelves in Fremantle.

Her immaculate looking sails were made from low weight laminated cloth, the by-product of a planned Russian/French space probe which called for a balloon to be launched from a rocket into the atmosphere of Venus where it would have to withstand the buffeting of winds of more than 200 knots.

Marc Pajot and his crew also brought style and grace to the America's Cup.

If the pink zinc lipped Frenchman took the message seriously he would wipe the smile off his countryman's face.

Overleaf: A sign of the times, the helmsman's name painted, motor racing style, on the side of the very professional French Kiss *effort.*

MARCH

As red as a Flander's poppy, the spinnaker of French Kiss *is packed for yet another race.*

Right: k1, p1, k2tog, 'has anyone seen the knitting pattern?'

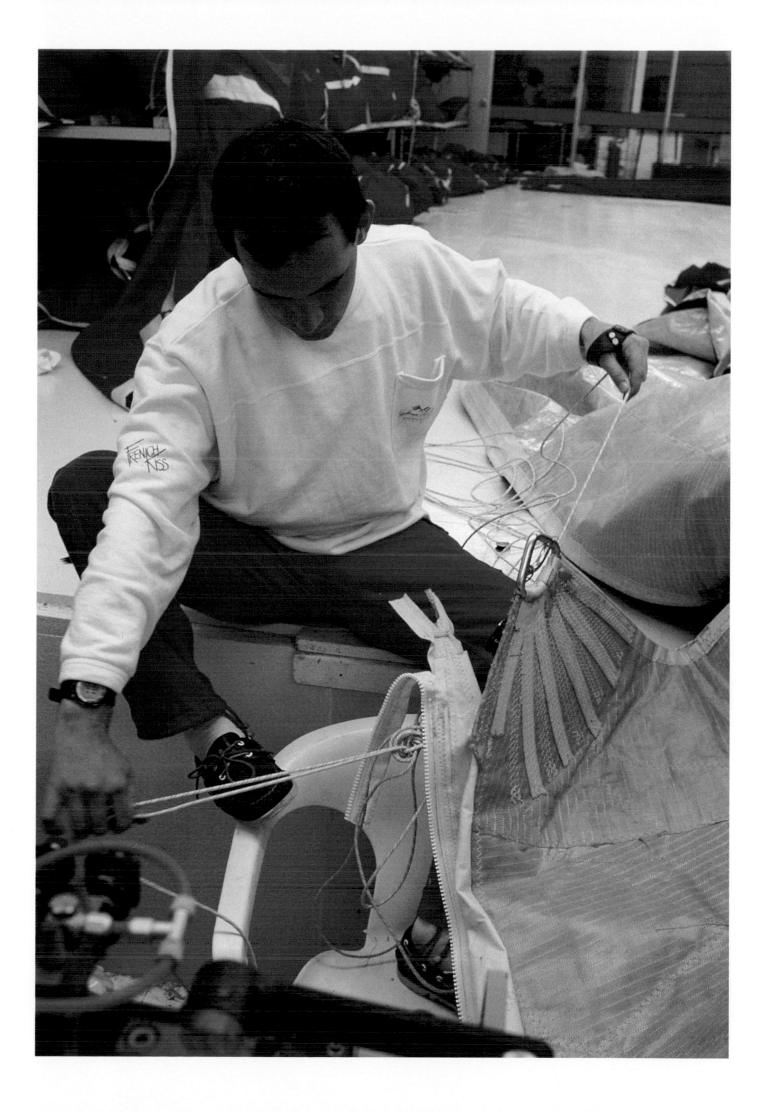

They had the best looking boat graphics and the T-shirts and windcheaters bearing them became the most sought after garments of the summer. Pajot's English was just good enough to communicate his sense of fun. When the skippers gathered to talk to the press about changes they had made to their boats after the first round robin, Pajot said: 'We spent a few times with our wives and our girlfriends and in this way think we improve our *French Kiss*. All the crew is determined to have a good second round robin.'

French Kiss did improve and, with consistent sailing, made the semi-finals as number four, opposed to the points leader *New Zealand 7*. But as the World Championship winner *Australia III* found, speed in February 1986 meant little against a general acceleration in performance, and in improving her light airs speed *French Kiss* sacrificed some of the brilliant heavy airs pace she had shown at the World Championship.

She went down in four straight races to *New Zealand 7* and was out of the competition. Serge Crasnianski, head of Kis, said that after the two wins in the World Championships the syndicate had decided to capitalise on this promising success by preparing one boat perfectly instead of hastily building a second 12-Metre. The syndicate had funds available which were comparable with those of the best challenges.

A struggle for funds stopped *USA*, the most innovative yacht of the regatta, developing to her full potential. Tom Blackaller, her ebullient fast-talking skipper, said the St. Francis Yacht Club based syndicate started so late, and without enough funds to compete against syndicates spending US$20 million, with an evolutionary boat that its only chance of winning was to develop the radical concept.

USA was designed by a team comprising aerodynamicist Alberto Calderon, yacht designer Gary Mull, computer science physicist Heiner Meldner and Alfred Buckingham, a computational fluid dynamicist, whose speciality is drag reduction on ship hulls.

Instead of a keel, *USA* had a huge, torpedo-shaped blob of lead, suspended

USA: *The outrageous design with the outrageous skipper. R1 was Tom Blackaller's radical stab at beating the system. R1's design featured a bow rudder, clearly seen here as the bow rises out of the water. A torpedo shape lead stabilizer suspended on a narrow support from the centre of the boat, and a deep stern rudder.*

by a slender aerofoil shaped stem, mainly to provide righting moment. Most of the lift, to stop the yacht from sliding sideways, was provided by a deep narrow aerofoil shaped 'rudder' ahead of the keel (it was about six feet deep and two feet wide) plus the usual steering rudder aft. Upwind, the bow foil's trailing edge was angled at two or three degrees to the water flow, lifting the bow to windward in opposition to the usual four or five degrees of rudder angle which also provided lift to windward by pulling the stern up and depressing the bow. This canard system, insisted Blackaller, was the idea of Calderon whose consultant design work in aerospace and aviation research included space vehicles, surveillance planes for the US Navy and the Concorde and Airbus airliners.

The steering system, to cope with the different angles of attack of the two rudders, both in straight line upwind sailing and in tacking, was extremely complicated. Blackaller spoke of the yacht 'spinning out' when it was going to windward and also said that the system did not have the feel of a regular yacht. The helmsman had to depend totally on the instruments. It was, he imagined, like steering an airliner.

Through the heat of the Fremantle summer the well-publicised, long-standing feud between Blackaller and Conner appeared to cool off; certainly at the press conferences where they even teamed up in the 'Glassgate' war against the Kiwis. Asked about it, Blackaller said he didn't like the 'bludgeon' tactics Conner uses to try to win races with three year US$15 million programmes. 'I don't think that is good for the sport. I don't think that proves anything about anything, if you just go out and get more money and spend more time, it becomes less of a sport and more like a business or maybe something like the US Government.

'Dennis has always been one of the people I respect greatly as a sailor; he is a top sailor. And I wish to hell he hadn't turned the sport into something where it costs you 20 million bucks to compete.'

USA, with her low drag underwater appendages, was very fast downwind,

More than a million words parted those lips and most of them were pearls. Blackaller, Levi dressed, in full flight.

and upwind at times was also high and fast. She beat Conner's *Stars & Stripes* twice in the rounds robin only to be swept off the board 4-0 in the final by a *Stars & Stripes* which, said Blackaller, found two tenths of a knot extra Vmg (Velocity made good) to windward.

Sydney-*Steak 'n' Kidney*, did not have the points to qualify for the defender finals when three races short of the end of the fourth series, and so was eliminated after her syndicate head, Syd Fischer, fought a running battle with the Royal Perth Yacht Club to have the points system changed to suit his improving yacht. Fischer argued that the fourth series should either be a true semi-final, as that for the challengers was, or to have the points score start afresh for it. He even took his fight with the club to the West Australian Supreme Court but, after *Steak 'n' Kidney* could not score the wins she needed in the final round robin to pursue that argument, dropped the action.

Fischer, unable to find the support he needed from corporate sponsors, largely funded the A$7 million from his own pocket. Peter Cole tested 20 designs at the Netherlands Ship Model Basin before finally selecting one he thought would be fast in all wind strengths. Cole also settled on two keels at the Wageningen facility but unfortunately chose the wrong one to put on the boat. *Steak 'n' Kidney*, too unstable in the first series, was slightly better in the second after a modification to the *French Kiss* style, aft swept keel Cole chose. In the third series, however, after the keel was cut up and re-poured by Fischer and his team in ten days – *Steak 'n' Kidney* was transformed.

Under small headsails, her slender looking, easily driven hull was the fastest of the defenders in 22 knots of wind and more; but the no-frills campaign was rough around the edges. She lost two probable wins, over *Australia IV* and *Kookaburra III*, with broken headsail halyards caused by collapsed bearings on sheaves in the mast. She also suffered from poor starts. Phil Thompson took over the helm from Fred Neill for the fourth series and experience was added to the crew by refugees from *Australia III* and *South Australia*.

Defiant Dennis Conner.

New Zealand 7's sound and polished first challenge campaign paid no heed to convention with the first glassfibre yacht in the America's Cup. It was the development of an identical pair by three designers who have won international acclaim for their ocean racing designs: Laurie Davidson, Bruce Farr and Ron Holland. The campaign was solidly financed, initially by merchant banker Michael Fay and thereafter by the Bank of New Zealand and other major sponsors whom he recruited. Fay, as syndicate chairman, continued to play a dominant role and was a frank and forthright spokesman for the Kiwis during the prolonged 'Glassgate' assault on the legality of *New Zealand 7's* glassfibre construction.

New Zealand 7's skipper, Chris Dickson, who turned 25 during the regatta, and celebrated it with a win over Dennis Conner led a strong young crew that remained close knit and impervious to the furore that at times surrounded their boat – in much the same way that *Australia II's* crew shut themselves off from the great winged keel controversy that was 'Keelgate' in 1983.

Dickson, who, said Ian Wooldridge of the London *Daily Mail,* had the piercing blue eyes and intensity of a World War II U-boat commander – a tag that stuck through the summer – withstood all the pressure applied not only by his opponents on the water, but also by the wave of support from three and a half million New Zealanders as their boat stayed on the top of the points table to the end of the rounds robin and then demolished *French Kiss* in the semi-finals. At press conferences he was asked over and over again about that pressure. 'Our whole team is a young team; our country is a young country. We take every race one at a time,' was a typical response.

His armour did crack in the final against the new found speed might of *Stars & Stripes* and a confident Conner. A crash gybe around the first leeward mark in the fourth race tore the electronic aerials from the transom and bent the top of the mast and a last desperate run in the fifth race ended with *New Zealand 7* hitting the buoy when within a boat's length of *Stars & Stripes.*

Suddenly older and wiser, Chris Dickson.

The ceremonial handing over of the Lipton trophy from the Royal Perth Yacht Club Commodore, Alan Crewe, to the San Diego Yacht Club Commodore, Fred Frye, in the presence of D.B. Johnston, Vice-Commodore of the Royal Ulster Yacht Club, Sir Thomas Lipton's challenging club.

Right: The only time the three 'plastic fantastics' sailed together was in this display of sponsor Bank of New Zealand's spinnakers.

On the defender course the Bond syndicate came to the end of the road, despatched 5-0 by a *Kookaburra III* that became suddenly faster with a keel change before the final. The syndicate which won the America's Cup made a tremendous contribution to its first defence with the same methodical approach and principal characters. Ben Lexcen's design progression stayed just a pace behind the three Kookaburras. Such was the speed of development for Fremantle that *Australia III,* the 12-Metre world champion of February 1986, was retired by the syndicate after the second series because she was uncompetitive and the syndicate preferred to put all its resources behind *Australia IV.*

Colin Beashel proved to be a cool and capable helmsman and with the 1983 veterans, tactician Hugh Treharne and navigator Grant Simmer, formed an afterguard that often out-foxed the Kookaburras. In the end, however, they were devastated by a faster boat.

Warren Jones, the syndicate's executive director, again played a shrewd psychological role with a continual needling of the Taskforce syndicate over its penchant for protests culminating in his famous 'they howl like dingoes when they are beaten,' comment. He retained his good humour in defeat and at the press conference following *Australia IV's* elimination said: 'I guess we have tasted and savoured victory and it's a poor Australian that cannot also taste and savour defeat. We have won in many ways and I can assure you that there are plenty of people back in our compound tonight who are far better people with the experience they have had over three years and by learning how to accept defeat. As individuals we have won.' Then Jones let out a weird call and explained: 'That is a wounded dingo and I am a wounded dingo.'

Kookaburra III, the product of a budget that began at A\$6.4 million and finally reached somewhere around A\$28 million, went into the America's Cup with a crew honed to match racing excellence by the tight competition with *Kookaburra II* and *Australia IV,* but with a vehicle which was 20 seconds slower on each beat to windward than the slightly more technically advanced design of *Stars & Stripes.*

Alan Bond was a keen if not always enthusiastic observer from Australia IV's *tender. The crew respected his perceptive input.*

Iain Murray, who directed the whole project and was co-designer with John Swarbrick as well as skippering *Kookaburra III,* was an inspiring leader of a young crew that had its foundations in the hapless *Advance* challenge of 1983. Peter Gilmour was an early recruit as project manager and after steering the bench mark boat *Kookaburra II,* to within two wins of making the defender final, went aboard *Kookaburra III* as starting helmsman.

The Taskforce syndicate adopted a low public profile compared to the Bond group and so there was shock and disbelief when its founder, chairman and underwriter Kevin Parry, gave Alan Bond a tongue lashing for the comments Bond made after the dismissal of *Australia IV:* 'Kevin, we brought the Cup here to Australia, don't you lose it,' (at the post-race press conference) and 'If Kevin doesn't defend it, we will have to go and get it back for you...' (before a cheering crowd at the Royal Perth Yacht Club's annexe).

Parry, at the press conference, gave a new insight into his tough, straight, no-nonsense nature with his put-down of Bond: 'I don't think the highest accolade can be paid to Alan Bond and his troops for bringing the America's Cup to Australia; but we're very sincere in what we set out to do; to give them either the best competition possible or help them achieve their greatest effort in defending the America's Cup that they brought to Australia.'

'However, I will not put up with any spite or nonsense. The fact is that we are entitled to defend through superior technology, through superior team work and through superior excellence; I think that has to be registered.' Turning to Bond, sitting two places from him, Parry continued: 'Frankly, Alan, I think your statement threw unnecessary pressure on us. We are out there to do our best and we are not prepared to put up with any needling or any spite. The fact that you weren't good enough in the run down to provide the competition is a fact of life. I don't think it is necessary to stand up at the Royal Perth Yacht Club annexe and say, "Well, we won it and if you lose it we'll have to go and get it back." I think that is childish, unnecessary and not worthy of your previous efforts.'

Peter Gilmour attacked the task of skippering Kookaburra II *with a school boy cheekiness which endeared him to his crew. Tactician Peter Hollis, behind him, enjoyed the association.*

Confrontation between the Bond syndicate and the Parry Taskforce syndicate after Kookaburra III *finally disposed of* Australia IV. *Executive Director Warren Jones flanked by Colin Beashel and Alan Bond responds to...*

...the stinging rebuke of Kevin Parry to a Bond remark. Parry said he was only speaking up for his skipper, Iain Murray (at right) and the Taskforce team.

The reaction to that statement, on the crest of a wave of sympathy for the defeated Bond group, did not swamp Parry who explained that he was speaking up for the hundred people working at Taskforce who were not allowed to answer back.

Through the America's Cup match public support rallied behind Murray and his crew; on the evening of their defeat they were mobbed as they left the dock and crowds of young Australians spent the night in Fremantle celebrating the defeat with the same intensity as the Americans in town celebrated *Stars & Stripes'* victory. 'I cannot fully explain it,' Murray said later, 'it's either somehow people relate to the group or they relate to me. I think it is a lot to do with the fact that we were always understated, always the underdogs, whether sailing against Bondy or Conner. I think that Australians have always been good at relating to underdogs and I guess that many, many people in the world are good at relating to underdogs. Their expectation of us wasn't that high, but we produced some good results. I'm pretty happy.'

Dennis Conner's *Stars & Stripes* syndicate rolled into Fremantle after two years of preparation in Hawaii without outward show of confidence. Conner, the master of the long, slow and expensive America's Cup preparation, had been struggling with his fund raising and some of the best developments from the most intensive research campaign ever undertaken into 12-Metre design were left sitting on the shelf.

Stung by the technological superiority of *Australia II* in 1983, Conner's San Diego Yacht Club based Sail America syndicate enlisted three designers: Britton Chance Jr., Bruce Nelson and David Pedrick; and surrounded them with teams of technical experts in computer aided design and tank testing, drawn from the aviation, aerospace, defence and ship-building industries, co-ordinated by John Marshall, the mainsheet trimmer of *Liberty* in the 1983 match. With a roster of five yachts, beginning with the 1983 defender and a rebuilt *Spirit of America,* the design ideas were tested full size in the steady 18-25 knot trade winds off Waikiki, Hawaii.

The first assault by the press.

Stars & Stripes' *design coordinator John Marshall brought together an enormous flow of technical assistance.*

The Stars & Stripes *design team from left: David Pedrick, Bruce Nelson, Britton Chance Jr.*

Overleaf: The smile on the face of the tiger — Dennis Conner confident in his boat speed.

But the training in isolation left Conner and his team without any true line on their speed until they reached Fremantle in July. Initially, in light weather, *Stars & Stripes* was painfully slow and she was still struggling in the early rounds robin with Conner saying 'If it stays light, we'll be home for Thanksgiving, let alone Christmas.'

Four defeats in the second round robin stung the syndicate and its designers into some significant improvements which probably won the America's Cup. The most dramatic game came from a winglet change. The boat was put into a lighter ballast configuration, the mast position was changed, and a deeper rudder was fitted to dampen the steering through the steep, short Gage Roads waves. New sails were made on the spot to overcome the lag between having a good idea in Fremantle produced by Lofts in the USA and then flown out for testing. Through the third round robin, where *Stars & Stripes* lost to *New Zealand 7* and *USA*, there was also the feeling that Conner was masking the improvement to his boat.

In the challenger final against *New Zealand 7,* however, and the match against *Kookaburra III,* Conner showed what he had a 12-Metre that could outpace any other upwind. She was equally able to foot for pace to escape a windward cover or point to blast off an opponent on her weather quarter with disturbed air. What shook the *Kookaburra* crew's notion that they had the fastest running Twelve in the fleet was the ability of *Stars & Stripes* to run well.

All of the match racing skills which Murray and his crews had developed through the defender eliminations were of no use against this speed edge. Conner said: 'It's a difficult problem when you have a boat like *Stars & Stripes* that won't play the match racing game. When we don't tack and we don't cover, its pretty hard for them to be aggressive and exploit the fact that they do tack better and manoeuvre better.'

Conner admitted that *Stars & Stripes* did not show all her cards at the beginning of the campaign. 'We are sailing this boat at least three tenths of a knot faster than we sailed *Liberty* last time. That's a major, major increase in speed.'

CHAPTER TWO

Defender and Challenger Eliminations

Defender Eliminations

Royal Perth Yacht Club, after consultation with the syndicates, devised the format of the defender eliminations so that from three rounds robin (Series A, B, C) of a total 105 races, the four top scoring yachts would go into Series D which, unlike the challenger semi-final, was also a round robin with the two scorers becoming the finalists.

However, two of the entries, *Australia III* and *South Australia,* eliminated themselves along the way and a third, *Sydney-Steak 'n' Kidney,* dramatically improved after a keel change between Series B and Series C, was fighting to accumulate enough points to make competing in Series D worthwhile.

After leading the points score at the end of the first three rounds robin, *Kookaburra III* was top qualifier for Series D with 53 points from *Australia IV* 47, *Kookaburra II* 34, and *Steak 'n' Kidney* 12.

The Taskforce syndicate's golden-hulled Kookaburras were always fast and very evenly matched. *Kookaburra II* was intended to be the bench-mark for *Kookaburra III.* She was left unaltered from May 1986 while heavy development work went into the hulls and keels of *Kookaburra III* and *Kookaburra I.*

Peter Gilmour, appointed her skipper, was really itching to get on to the same boat as Iain Murray. He had been with the syndicate from its beginnings in 1984 as Project Manager and wanted to cement a place in the America's Cup crew.

But at the helm of *Kookaburra II,* he immediately stamped himself on the regatta as its most aggressively fearless starter. His hair trigger reactions and sheer unpredictability kept his competitors on edge. Backing him was a strong afterguard – Peter Hollis, tactician, who defected from the Bond syndicate because he could not fill that spot there, and Andrew York as navigator. The crew was an experienced bunch but most of them had spent the weeks before the regatta toiling at Parry Boatbuilders, virtually rebuilding *Kookaburra I* as

Kookaburra II *leading* Kookaburra III *in full size testing of hull/keel shapes.*
Previous page: In her early races New Zealand 7 *was totally dominant. Here she leads* USA *by a substantial margin.*
Overleaf: Kookaburra III *setting up for the wing mark gybe under typical pressure from fast reaching* Australia IV.

Heavy traffic on the congested Roads. Kookaburra III *crossing* Australia IV*: South Australia *alongside* Australia III.

The wounded crow, South Australia, *with band-aid over the wound inflicted by* Steak 'n' Kidney.

Overleaf: Sheltering behind the bulk of Iain Murray, tactician Derek Clark peers into Kookaburra III's *tactical computer display. Under the scrutiny of 'racecam', the on-board television camera that put the crew into living rooms across the world.*

well as honing *Kookaburra II* and *Kookaburra III*. But from the ragged beginnings, they clicked into an efficient unit with wonderful cameraderie.

Kookaburra III was the yacht the syndicate wanted to win through to the finals with *Kookaburra II* in second place to shut out the Bond syndicate's *Australia IV*. But the speed of *Kookaburra II* set off a collective attack of head-scratching within the syndicate. Until a keel modification to *Kookaburra III* after Series D, Murray believed *Kookaburra II* was the faster boat. The admissions will never be made publicly, but when the two Kookaburras raced during the first three rounds robin, *Kookaburra III* was always to win. Murray and his afterguard – Derek Clark, tactician, and Ian Burns, navigator – were distracted somewhat from the racing by the roles they also had in developing the design and technology of both yachts. While they had their heads only partially extracted from the computers, Gilmour and his more carefree crowd were able to just get on with the job of sailing their boat. Murray's own sailing was to improve significantly when Gilmour came on board as starting helmsman for the defender final after *Australia IV* beat *Kookaburra II* for the final spot.

Australia IV began the eliminations on the back foot. Although she had even speed with the Kookaburras, they were out-tacking her in Series A – faster to tack, or at least able to come out on a higher line and accelerate more quickly after a tack.

Gradually Colin Beashel and his crew overcame that deficiency. *Australia IV's* designer Ben Lexcen felt the tacking advantage of the Kookaburras was due to the close nature of the racing they had been having in their preparation for the regatta rather than to anything in the hull design or on-board instrumentation. Lexcen added a very fine 'canard' fin, running between the leading edge tip of *Australia IV's* heavily-bulbed wing keel and the hull before Series B. And the combination of the faster *Australia IV* and the more confident crew allowed them to keep splitting the Kookaburras at the head of the points table.

Fight for control in a pre-start. Kookaburra II *and* Australia IV.

Don McCracken, Kookaburra III's *bowman, just loved being at the top of the mast. Here he is, sawing the mainsail away from a broken headboard carriage.*

Left: Kookaburra III *and* Kookaburra II *cutting figures in a pre-start waltz.*

Overleaf: Heavy black sail trim reference stripes readily identified the Kookaburras. They were used for computer driven analysis of sail shapes.

The win by *Australia IV* over *Kookaburra III* on day six of Series A, the only defeat of the Taskforce syndicate's flagship in that series, was to establish a pattern for the later racing. *Australia IV* won the start by three seconds and that became the winning advantage. In the final few seconds to the gun, with the yachts side by side, *Kookaburra III* to windward, *Australia IV* was a fraction earlier sheeting on sails and accelerating for the line. The mainsheet trim came on a little too quickly on *Kookaburra III* which drove the bow up, slowing the boat instead of allowing helmsman Murray to drive off for the line with smooth acceleration.

Australia IV rounded the first mark 20 sec ahead and had 15 sec in hand at the end of the first run when *Kookaburra III* immediately attacked with a brisk tacking duel. *Australia IV* broke from the pattern by stretching out her tacks on starboard and slamming a hard cover on port over *Kookaburra III* each time Murray tried to take *Australia IV's* stern.

The strategy of Beashel and his tactician, Hugh Treharne, and navigator, Grant Simmer, with the yachts so even in speed, were to deny *Kookaburra III* any chance of getting out to the right and being on the right-of-way starboard tack on the final approach to the windward mark. Again and again, with the split of tacks often wide, that pattern was repeated – a test of nerve as well as sailing skill and judgement. *Australia IV* was only nine seconds ahead at the second windward mark, her tactics were identical on the third and fourth windward beats, she won by 36 sec and from that race, the strategy of strenuously protecting the right became dominant in the defender eliminations.

Australia III, the winner of the World Championship off Fremantle just eight months before, was a disappointment right from the start of Series A, able to beat only *South Australia* and *Steak 'n' Kidney*. The Bond syndicate insisted she was still a fine all-rounder; doing her job of covering the lower end of the wind range where *Australia IV* was vulnerable. The implication was that skipper Gordon Lucas with his tactician, Carl Ryves, and his navigator, Nigel

Australia IV *shows off her maximum width keel wing. Aerial photography gave strong hints of secrets shrouded ashore.*

Overleaf: Bowman Greg Johnson wrestles with wet uncooperative Kevlar sailcloth on Kookaburra II.

Abbott, were making mistakes, but Lucas just didn't have the confidence in the boat and so did not sail well.

The Bond syndicate withdrew *Australia III* from the competition at the end of Series B when the scoreboard was: *Kookaburra III* 29, *Australia IV* 20, *Kookaburra II* 19, *Australia III* 12, *South Australia* 8, *Steak 'n' Kidney* 0. The Bond syndicate reasoned she had been surpassed by the next generation of Twelves like *Australia IV* and the two Kookaburras and wanted to concentrate all its resources on *Australia IV*.

South Australia, one per cent faster than her competitors downwind but four per cent slower upwind through Series A, added bigger wings to her keel for Series B. Phil Thompson steered the boat well and John Savage's tactics were correct. The boat just lacked upwind speed in all conditions any time there were waves about.She scored an upset win over *Australia IV* by 1:36, on the last day of racing in Series B – no great surprise as the breeze never rose above nine knots and the sea was dead flat, conditions in which *South Australia* had always been fast. But on that day, the SA syndicate announced she had been sold to Swedish yachtsmen Thomas Wallin and Lars Brostrom, with Sweden's former America's Cup skipper Pelle Peterson negotiating the deal. *South Australia* bent her mast and retired before the start of her day four match in Series C against *Australia IV* and the syndicate pulled her out of the competition.

Although *South Australia* looked to have reached the end of her development road, *Steak 'n' Kidney* certainly had some distance left but not enough time. She began the elimination with the wrong keel. During his tank testing program at the Netherlands Ship Model Basin, Peter Cole tried two designs that both showed promise: an 'upside down' keel with big wings like the one carried on *Australia II* and a swept-back International Offshore Rule style keel with small winglets. After *French Kiss* showed great promise in the Twelve Metre World Championship with a similar keel Cole chose the swept-back keel. But the boat did not have enough stability with this keel, despite

Kookaburra III *leads* Steak 'n' Kidney. *Sydney's yacht's more slender shape was a disadvantage on the reaching legs.*

South Australia *leads* Australia III *from the wrong side of the Committee Boat to start after an aggressive run through the spectactors.*

'We won today.' South Australia, *facing a hopeless task, hung together with fine crew spirit.*

Overleaf: The Kookaburras shed their feathers for another close leeward mark rounding.

a reshaping of the keel root and the addition of bigger winglets as an expediency in the short break between Series A and Series B.

In the longer break between Series B and Series C, syndicate head Syd Fischer, Cole and their team cut up the keel and repoured it into the upside down shape of Cole's original testing with a bulbed bottom and wings modified, according to Fischer, by 'what we have been able to pick up around the traps in Fremantle.' It was similar to *Kookaburra II's* (they were cast in the same foundry).

The Sydney yacht began Series C with a 5:54 win over *South Australia* in a fresh, 18-26 knot breeze. The following day *Steak 'n' Kidney* confirmed that the new keel had made her into a heavy air flier. In a 23-28 knot breeze, looking extremely efficient under her little 'blade', code six, jib and flat mainsail, she outsailed *Australia IV* on all windward legs except the one that mattered most – the last. Around the last mark, *Steak 'n' Kidney* led by 30 seconds. The train of events that was to prove her undoing was already rolling along. The code six jib had washed overboard on the last run. Skipper Neill was confident about hanging onto the code five up to the last beat but soon after the mark rounding, the halyard broke. The crew, after a struggle, rehoisted the sail on another halyard but the code five, as it was sheeted on, blew itself to bits. *Australia IV* went past to win by 2:46.

On day four, when she was only seven seconds behind *Kookaburra III* in 16-18 knots and, on the last beat, sliding along to what could have been a lee bow situation soon after the mark rounding, she again broke headsail halyard and finished under mainsail only, 1:52 behind *Kookaburra III*. When the mast was pulled out the following day and the masthead dismantled, the headsail halyard sheaves were found to be jammed because of collapsed axle bearings. That had caused the halyards to chafe and break.

Steak 'n' Kidney finally beat *Kookaburra II* twice in Series C to confirm the promise of her new keel and the belief that she might be the fastest of all the defenders in the winds above 22 knots.

Phil Thompson, after the retirement of South Australia, *was recruited to skipper* Steak 'n' Kidney. *He steered her with aggression and skill.*

Challenger Eliminations

The Yacht Club Costa Smeralda, in association with all the challenging syndicates, structured the races to reduce the challengers to four semi-finalists. In order to reward those boats which improved as the summer progressed, the points for the three rounds were progressively increased, one for a win in the first round, five in the second and twelve in the last. The top four on points, at the end, became the semi-finalists for the Louis Vuitton Cup.

The first round saw little but muscle flexing; yet at the end of it there were three boats level, each of which had lost only one race: *America II, New Zealand 7* and *Stars & Stripes.* The writing, in small letters, was already on the wall.

At the end of the round the challengers were reduced from thirteen to twelve; the elderly *Courageous* was withdrawn a day after she had won her last race. The Cup defender of 1974 and 1977 beat *Challenge France,* her only win in Australia.

An undefeated round by Chris Dickson and the Kiwi crew of *New Zealand 7* was the outstanding feat of the second round robin. The young Kiwi skipper gave himself the best possible 25th birthday present during the series. A quarter of a century of life was capped with a win over Dennis Conner in a 12-Metre match race and there could be very few things any yachtsmen could ask for to bring them greater happiness.

The Kiwis' success was the result of a very dedicated group of yachtsmen and the shore-based organisation together with the deeply rooted patriotic fervour that seems to incite Kiwis to higher things. Theirs was very definitely a united effort. They stood behind the party line; they had their own press conferences and they were in Fremantle to prove that there are Kiwis who were in Australia with a real purpose.

By the time that the Kiwi crew had been at the 12-Metre game for a year, they had taken a systematic approach to organising every manoeuvre on the

Nothing was too much for the Kiwi crew who went to the limit to make their boat the fastest on the water.

When New Zealand *met* Stars & Stripes *for the first time the weather swung wildly, turning beats into reaches – and Gage Roads was anything but friendly.*

Contrast in bow profiles. America II *and* Canada II.

Early in the summer Chris Dickson and his Kiwis had the edge over Conner and his Californians.

Left: White Crusader, *the natural development design from Ian Howlett, which took account of his* Victory '83 *and the breakthrough* Australia II *to provide a good all round boat which was eliminated by gear failure and mistakes.*

Overleaf: Action time on French Kiss *as Marc Pajot swings her on to starboard tack.*

The crews of French Kiss *and* Heart of America *walking on water as they approach the leeward mark.*

Right: The angry Eagle *punching waves before the start.*

Overleaf: 'We lost today, but we won't lose the next time we meet them.' A thoughtful Dennis Conner in defeat.

boat. The result was that their sailing appeared to be a totally cohesive effort and the boat moved through every one of their manoeuvres without fuss. Dickson could therefore concentrate on making her go through the water fast rather than having to worry if anything he wished to pull off might fail. The added confidence gave the youngest skipper in the series time to consider his moves carefully and thereby reduced mistakes to a bare minimum.

The disappointment of the second round robin was that of Dennis Conner. The world's best match racer in 12-Metres was doing his best to dispel the truth of that title. It wasn't his fault, unless you can blame him for having a boat optimised for heavy airs and a shortage of sails for the lighter breezes. Dennis was looking at the far end of the competition and was caught out when the spell of easterlies settled over the area. He lost on the first day to Tom Blackaller (and how that must have rankled) in 5/10 knot winds and the following day to Dickson when the breeze was up to 20 knots, and the Australian press began to write him off.

On the ninth day Conner lost to *White Crusader* around a 10 mile course by 2:18 in 4/6 knots of wind and not too many were surprised. The following day he lost to *Canada II*. After leading around the final mark, Conner succumbed to Terry Neilson as the wind died away. On the last day of the racing, however, the old Conner returned. In 22 knots of breeze he tore the heart out of *America II*. John Kolius led across the starting line but when the two boats came together for the first time Conner was level and from then on the issue was never in doubt. Conner had proved his point.

America II had only been beaten once before – when she met *New Zealand 7* – a new keel had been fitted and Kolius said that it was slower than the previous one. *America II* entered the third round robin in her 23rd configuration of the summer.

White Crusader's progress was one of ups and downs. She made heavy weather of beating *Canada II* in 17 knots of breeze, going to the front only on the final leg to record the closest ever winning margin in the history of the

A win for Blackaller in the duel of the summer.

One of the features of the Cup summer was the duel between Conner of Stars & Stripes *and Blackaller of* U.S.A.

Canada II, *Bruce Kirby's re-design which promised much but failed to deliver by the short margins which marked winners from losers.*

America's Cup. The record books will always say that it was one second but the Seiko timers were 29 hundredths of a second different! The loss of a mast when they were leading *USA* in what later appeared to have been a crucial match, was a serious set-back for the British effort.

A sad piece of yachting history was made on the tenth day of the third round robin when *America II* was eliminated from the selection series as she could no longer score enough points to qualify for the semi-finals. The New York Yacht Club would not contest the America's Cup final for the first time for 135 years.

White Crusader had gone two days earlier when she was defeated by a mere six seconds by *New Zealand 7* although the evidence was there for all to see in her previous match which she lost to *America II,* a race she should have won easily.

The demise of two of the leading contenders came as the result of grave errors of judgement in only tiny things which added up to disaster; *America II's* were in design, while *White Crusader's* were of timing. There just wasn't the depth of design talent for the New York Yacht Club's $20 million effort and whatever alterations were made to US 46 in between the second and third rounds robin were detrimental – she appeared to be slower. The lack of time available to the British Challenge meant that *White Crusader* was always a month behind her true potential and that her crew were not as good as they might have been with another month's practice; in turn these two shortfalls led to hurried decision making while racing, and that led to gear failure which in its turn converted probable wins into losses.

A protest that Blackaller had replaced a front rudder of *USA* after one had broken, took all day but was rejected as the international jury decided that the rule was there to stop changes such as those Conner had made using a triple certificate in 1983, and not to stop a replacement for damage, even though that was how the rule was written. Blackaller's continuous improvement of his radical boat until its performance matched the best, would point to other

John Kolius skippered America II, *the man of whom one syndicate head was heard to say 'You ain't heard the last of this boy yet.'*

Overleaf: Muscle and mind combine to produce a fast 12-Metre.

Azzurra *and* Eagle, *two boats for whom there were high hopes but only low performance.*

Right: The end for Challenge France. *Yves Pajot's syndicate didn't come back for the last few races of round robin three, following this disaster.*

Overleaf: The Kiwi magic of New Zealand 7.

syndicates pursuing this style in future America's Cups.

The Kiwis continued their all conquering path to the semi-finals, but they might easily have lost to *White Crusader*; the British boat led around every one of the marks and was only overtaken on the final beat. It was quite the best match of the entire series, if for nothing else, for the luffing match on the first reach which saw the Kiwis facing the direction from whence they had come, a smashed spinnaker boom and the crew caught flat-footed for the first time in the series.

The really marked improvement in this round was that of *Heart of America*. Buddy Melges decided to add tiplets to his winglets and go for broke by optimising for fresh breezes; the change was dramatic and the boat which had one time been an embarrassment for Buddy and incidentally all who have known him in the past, suddenly became alive and started to despatch the serious competition.

Canada II lacked the early promise she had shown. It may have been in the lack of time at her disposal but it certainly didn't suppress the enthusiasm of the group who were the first to come through with a definite statement that they would be back in the competition next time, no matter where it was to be held.

Italia seemed troubled by the loss of skipper Aldo Migliaccio, who was injured in a car accident. She showed flashes of speed, especially in the lighter breezes, but lacked downwind ability. *Azzurra*, from the Challenger of Record, the third boat to bear the name, was another which was troubled by a lack of boat speed and was never seriously in the hunt.

Neither was Yves Pajot's *Challenge France* which only had success when her opponents, both in the first round, broke down. *Challenge France* pulled out before the end of the third round when her mast broke. Yves' brother Marc, by contrast, developed the early potential of *French Kiss* and came strong when it was most needed, scoring points in the later rounds. In the third round she lost only to the three boats which finished above her and, strangely, *Italia*.

CHAPTER THREE

Behind Closed Doors

Behind Closed Doors

The 26th Defence of the America's Cup left in its wake the normal amount of broken marriages, wrecked careers and general abandonment but there were a host of other things which went on behind closed doors. The real age of secrecy began in 1983 but in Fremantle the screens were bigger and even less penetrable than they had been in Newport. Where once there was only one, now they had proliferated like daisies on a summer lawn. Only three of the nineteen contenders were without modesty skirts throughout the Cup summer: *Courageous, Challenge France* and *Heart of America;* keel technology was considered to be too important to share.

How right that was too. *Steak 'n' Kidney* was no threat until Peter Cole chanced upon the maximum wing span theory. The one he fitted to the Sydney boat looked remarkably like that of the Kookaburras' late model and transformed her performance dramatically.

Keels were often changed between series and more lies than truths were told about changes. There is evidence however that two men changed the keel on a 12-Metre, unaided, in four hours. That, of course, without the fairing that is always necessary and thanks too to the perfect alignment of the bolts with the frame structure in the hull. *America II,* with her 'Lego' keels, was often altered overnight during training periods, though exactly what went on was kept a strict secret by Cap'n Tuna, Arthur Wullschleger. Some of the changes necessitated visits out of the compounds to builders sheds but the majority were in-house affairs.

Perhaps the biggest of the in-house alterations was the one to *White Crusader* between the second and third rounds robin. A new, prefabricated bow section was flown from her British builder and the deck raised. The keel was lowered and a fillet placed between it and the hull while the counter was trimmed of its foam underbody. In addition the wings on the keel were changed and the maximum width bronze wings were raked further aft; it was

'Happy Birthday, Dennis.'

Previous page: Skilled bowmen were second pairs of eyes to helmsmen judging starting line approaches.

'If only we had more time.' Steak 'n' Kidney's *designer, Peter Cole, on her tender* Gazebelle.

Right: Cap'n Tuna, alias Arthur Wullschleger, the tyrannical dock boss for America II, *rumoured to have a heart...of gold.*

Overleaf: Smoothing the bow of Azzurra *after minor alterations to remove hollows.*

what dock boss 'Spud' Spedding referred to as the grandest of his Royal Tournaments.

Minor alterations went on all the time and *Australia IV* found her way back to Steve Ward's shed on a couple of occasions when the cutting torch and the welding gear were needed and a booking there kept *Steak 'n' Kidney* out when Syd Fischer wanted to change her shape.

Kookaburra III had her aft overhang fined down before the final trials began but that was not a problem for the Parry boatbuilders led by Toby Richardson. Their in-house operations had spawned other businesses as the three year programme wove its course.

Cut-off sterns became commonplace; even *Stars & Stripes* went in for surgery and had her tail docked. The result was not unpleasant but the one to *French Kiss* was; with uncharacteristic lack of aestheticism the French transformed one of the more elegant yachts on the water to the ugliest beyond doubt. Designer Philippe Briand must have wept at the savagery.

One boat even got arrested. *Courageous,* the grand old lady who had won the Cup twice, was the subject of an Admiralty Warrant which arrested her for the alleged non-payment of fees for her support boat, the owners of which were a trifle premature in their action – the bill did not fall due until some days after the arrest. The Perth Supreme Court struck out the writ and *Courageous* was allowed to go free.

Having an Admiral in the camp was a definite plus for the Brits (the *French Kiss* camp had one as well) and he did much to defuse the controversy over the ban of casting keels for challengers in Australia. His argument, that the keel was not part of the hull as much as a bolted-on appendage, finally won favour, a fact which might have saved the New York Yacht Club many dollars in air freight for the one which it had flown out from Connecticut – the freight charges were four times that of the keel itself!

One of the more interesting facets of the Cup summer was that the two finalists each employed its nation's Olympic coach, and what was more

French Kiss *wetting her lips.*

Overleaf: Just some of the sponsor spinnakers which Dennis Conner flew on the way home each day in the Finals.

important, listened to what they had to say. Mike Fletcher's role was acknowledged very early in the summer when he received the first of the Betts & Betts Achievement Awards. He and his chase boat were a familiar sight on Gage Roads, as was Robert Hopkins in his 'rubber ducky'; certainly when *Kookaburra III* put in some training with *New Zealand 7* immediately after the golden hulled boat was chosen to defend the Cup, Hopkins was there between them.

A year before the Cup, *Challenge France* ran into some financial difficuties and their shore operations manager, Laurent Esquier, was left behind. With no job and no income he was soon snapped up by the New Zealanders and strengthened their campaign beyond measure. Kiwi crew members who saw him chatting up girls at social functions were not averse to giving him a hard time by shouting to him, 'Come off it, Larry, stop putting on that bogus French accent.'

Crew life was heavily regimented by some syndicates – physical fitness was seen as a prime need, even the skippers were not excused – others were slightly more tolerant of human needs. Relaxation was often found on the 'way home from work' at the Norfolk Hotel. Crews found it a pleasant meeting place, but so too did the 'racer chasers' and it was a generally crowded place to socialise. Others went to the Straggler's Bar at Lombardos; there wasn't a long way for the Kookaburra and Stars & Stripes crews to walk for that. Bond syndicate sailors made their headquarters at the Primavera while the French and Italians found their delights at Gino's.

The high rollers had plenty of options too; many new places sprang up to serve the rich. The British felt there would be a need for a gentleman's club and established such a facility in the Crusader Yacht Club, one which is to continue long after the Cup has gone to San Diego. Casa Italia was created in the old Navy Club by Gucci and the place was redolent of style, so too was the Club Le Maschere, the Ciga Hotels answer for the Yacht Club Costa Smeralda.

The travellers were cared for by Ansett who founded a Golden Keel Club,

Cheerful to the end of the world's longest regatta, Commandante Gianfranco Alberini of Yacht Club Costa Smeralda, organiser of the challenger eliminations.

Previous page: With jib tack patch reminiscent of the crown of the Statue of Liberty, Stars & Stripes *powers to windward.*

Headsail for the day has been selected and the crewmen wrestle it on deck.

A moment of symbolic friendship: Alan Bond hands Iain Murray a 'Boxing Kangaroo' battle flag. It was never flown.

on the lines of their well known Golden Wing lounges at the airports. It looked out over Challenger Harbour and on race mornings John Bertrand provided incisive insight to what was in store that day.

Everyone got in on the act while the Cup races were in progress and surely that is why the America's Cup was the success that it was. At the Essex Restaurant you could even obtain a drink named after a Cup journalist and the media men were not slow to find the best food in town.

Parties were numerous and sometimes overlapped. The America's Cup Ball was filled to capacity and there were several hundred more who went to the Alternative Ball on the beach at Arthur's Head. Kookaburra had a ball, the Kiwis had a ball, Stars & Stripes had a party, the Royal Thames Yacht Club held a dinner, the Royal Perth Yacht Club had an enormous cocktail party under the stars while Louis Vuitton, who sponsored the challenger races, gave a mega-sized bash at the Royal Freshwater Bay Yacht Club. As at every other Cup in history, hangovers were frequent for those who tended to over-indulge.

It wasn't all sailing under cloudless skies; there was one fly in the ointment, the issue which became known as 'Glassgate'. In 1983 the fight between the New York Yacht Club and the Bond syndicate over the legality of the design of *Australia II's* winged keel was dubbed 'Keelgate'; the big issue of legality this time was that of the glassfibre construction of the three New Zealand 12-Metres. Conner opened the batting by saying that he thought they couldn't be legal and on a now famous evening at a Media Conference went on record as saying: 'There have been 78 12-Metres built, all in aluminium. Why would you want to build one in glass, unless you wanted to cheat.' It provoked the comment from Tom Blackaller, 'Oh no, he shouldn't have said that.'

Conner, and others, argued that the performance of the boat was enhanced by a construction which made the hull, contrary to the class rules, lighter than the equivalent boat in aluminium alloy so that it would be stiffer as the additional weight was in lead in the keel. In addition they claimed that

In training only, commercialism stamped its inevitable images on the Cup boats. Next time...

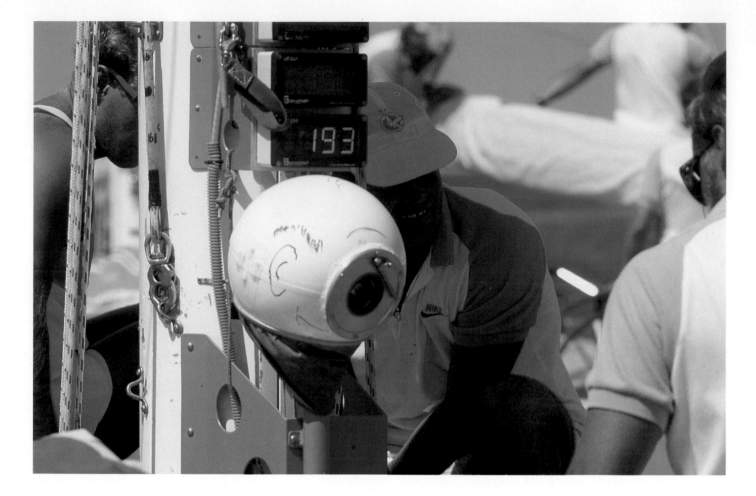

The all seeing eye on Kookaburra III *that took television audiences around the world on board with the crew.*

Right: Dickson and Son.

Lucy Jewitt, one of Conner's backers, with syndicate head Malin Burnham.

Left: Old Glory for Adam Ostenfeld.

there was less material used at the bow and the stern to reduce the radius of gyration and thereby the pitching. Conner wanted core samples taken of the hull to prove whether or not it had been correctly built. Michael Fay, the New Zealand syndicate head, consistently refused to allow this, saying that it would destroy the integral structure of the boat.

All the time the Kiwis maintained that the boat was legal. A Lloyds Register of Shipping surveyor was present throughout the construction of the boats and he checked each part of the laminate and the amount and type of resin used against the building schedule which Lloyds had approved. *New Zealand 7* was twice measured and twice certificated by Lloyds before the first race of the series but there were those who still challenged the legality of the boat; the French Kiss syndicate threatened to take the matter to the New York State Supreme Court, which they appeared to regard as the legal arbiter. The moment that the ten minute gun fired for the first race of their semi-final match with the Kiwis, a protest flag was broken out on *French Kiss*. The International Jury dismissed the protest and when the French withdrew their last ditch threat, the matter was settled – the three boats were definitely unchallenged legal 12-Metres.

They were all the time and when *New Zealand 7* was finally measured some small holes, definitely not core samples, were drilled in the hull simply to check the thickness. The hull was also ultra-sonically examined to check for any patches of air built into the hull and all proved negative. In the end Conner gave up his witchhunt, probably because he believed that he was faster anyway.

It was the one serpent in the Garden, providing lots of copy for the huge army of media people in Fremantle. The facilities provided in the IBM Media Centre, in the appropriately named Fleet Street, were so good that many with almost impossible deadlines never left the building in their coverage of the Cup. Which was their loss because they would have missed the other boats that were out on Gage Roads watching the protagonists.

A touch of Kiwi magic.

Tight security at the Royal Perth Yacht Club's specially built measuring pen.

Left: Paper work for a new sail. Measurer Ken McAlpine watches after measurement.

Overleaf: Ken McAlpine steers Kookaburra II *into the scrutineering dock for check measurement after a race. Murray and crew seem unconcerned, but are they?*

The spectator catamarans, many from the Tasmanian builder, International Catamarans, carried thousands afloat during the summer while there were some startling craft among the syndicates' fleet. The prize for the ugliest but most efficient tender must go to Conner for *Betsy,* the surface piercing catamaran; that for sheer ostentation must have to be split because there were so many but Alan Bond must figure highly for upstaging his own *Southern Cross II* with an even more lavish *Southern Cross III.* The officers of the Royal Perth Yacht Club were not far behind with their chartered *Parts VI* and there was *Carmac* and *Enterprise III* from two American syndicates and the delightful Camper & Nicholson designed *Rampager* which must have been the prettiest of the motor yachts. There were big sail boats too; Bill Packer's *Scotch Mist* took pride of place until *Freedom* out-did her, while from the pages of yachting records there were Jim Kilroy's *Kialoa III* and Conny van Rietschoten's *Flyer,* the winner of the Whitbread Round the World Race, both now converted for cruising. It was a dazzling display.

CHAPTER FOUR

Defender and Challenger Semi-Finals and Finals

Defender Semi-Finals and Finals

After the dust settled from the usual protest hearing, *Kookaburra III* emerged from Series D, the last of the rounds robin as points leader on 83 from *Australia IV* 77, *Kookaburra II* 70. *Steak 'n' Kidney*, 24, was eliminated three races from the end for not having enough points to reach the final as required by Royal Perth Yacht Club's condition for the regatta.

Phil Thompson, who helmed South Australia in the earlier rounds robin steered *Steak 'n' Kidney* in Series D. Her last race was her best. In a 17-20 knot sou'wester that gusted to 30 towards the end of the race, she led *Kookaburra III* around every mark to win by 39 seconds. Syd Fischer, who had funded the Sydney yacht almost totally with his own money, made it available to the Bond syndicate as a pace boat for *Australia IV* in the finals.

Kookaburra II scored five wins and three losses in Series D while *Kookaburra III* and *Australia IV* each won four and lost four. The racing between the three was always extremely close and so became aggressive and acrimonious, with many protests. On day three, *Kookaburra II* and *Australia IV* had a minor collision during the pre-start manoeuvres. *Kookaburra II*, after gaining a 12 second jump on the starting line, led around all marks to win by 29 seconds and win again in the protest with the jury disqualifying *Australia IV* under Rule 39.1 (when overlapped, a windward yacht shall keep clear of a leeward yacht).

On day five, *Australia IV*, after winning the start by 12 seconds and leading all the way, lost a certain win over *Kookaburra III* when the stitching inside webbing holding the mainsail to its headboard broke and the mainsail fell down. In the five minutes it took the *Australia IV* crew to repair the webbing and rehoist the mainsail, *Kookaburra III* went by to a 17 second win.

Australia IV, now struggling to make the defender final, the following day unleashed the genniker, her massive reaching spinnaker built within the balloon jib paragraph of the 12-Metre rule which is vague on the measurement

Previous page: Seldom more than a boat's length apart, Australia IV *and* Kookaburra III *had razor edge racing in the semi-finals.*

Gybing the genniker always meant a trip up the mast for Kookaburra III's *bowman Don McCracken to unplait the halyards.*

Overleaf: The Kookaburras at play. Headsail foreground, held back deliberately to push the bow away in a fast tack.

limitations. The Bond syndicate's sailmaking team headed by Tom Schnackenberg had developed the sail over many weeks of testing in secrecy at sea with the intention of keeping it for the Cup match.

But, with *Kookaburra II* 13 seconds ahead on the first reach, *Australia IV* set this very wide assymetrical sail with a single luff, like the spinnaker of an 18ft skiff. The powerful bodied *Australia IV* was sensationally fast under this new sail but as she ranged up to pass *Kookaburra II* to windward, Gilmour luffed sharply and *Kookaburra II's* spinnaker pole speared into the genniker and split it vertically in half. With half the sail, *Australia IV* was still fast and, after changing to a regular spinnaker, rounded the wing mark ahead and went on to finish 41 seconds ahead. But she lost the race in the protest room on two counts – not responding sufficiently to the luff to avoid contact and at the wing mark for failing to give *Kookaburra II,* the inside overlapping yacht, room to round. *Kookaburra III,* on day seven, won her way into the final with a win over *Kookaburra II*. She was handed a 15 second break on the starting line. The usually aggressive Gilmour unaccountably broke off his control of *Kookaburra III* in the last minute to the gun when she was completely vulnerable, with a man up the mast trying to close a burst mainsail luff zipper.

Australia IV looked well beaten by *Kookaburra II* the next day (day eight) in light winds, only six to eight knots early in the race and she was 2:17 behind around the third windward mark. She used her genniker to stay in touch and, on the second reach, turned square by a general swing in the wind direction, came down on the streak of new breeze to round the second leeward mark 45 seconds behind. Almost as soon as *Australia IV* rounded the mark, the wind shifted another 30 degreess to the left and started to freshen. *Kookaburra II,* gradually lifting from the mark-rounding and believing she could lay straight to the windward mark, did not tack back across *Australia IV* to try and cover her. *Australia IV* lifted inside *Kookaburra II* and, with first use of the fresher breeze, steadily improved her situation. With her beamy hull shape and heavy keel, she was able to extract more power from her light air sails with the wind

Australia IV's *genniker, a powerful secret weapon in her armoury could not save her from final defeat.*

Overleaf: Messy late spinnaker drop gave Kookaburra III *crew all sorts of problems while* Australia IV *gratefully accepted the two boat length breathing space.*

increasing to 14-16 knots and she laid straight to the third windward mark on port tack to round 10 seconds ahead of *Kookaburra II* which had to make a 100 yard tack on starboard back to the mark. *Australia IV* went on to win by 24 seconds but then had to face a protest about the way she had flown the genniker from a three foot strop while gybing and changing sails. That was to lead to a deadlock situation broken only by the summit meeting between Alan Bond, Kevin Parry and the Royal Perth Yacht Club.

The day nine race between *Australia IV* and *Kookaburra III* was another close encounter that became too close when they collided on the second windward leg. The collision left *Kookaburra III* with a ragged hole in her bow and *Australia IV* with a scar in her topsides on the aft starboard quarter. *Australia IV* led around all marks after Beashel won the start, controlling Murray out beyond the starboard tack layline to the committee boat end. *Kookaburra III* was a shade faster upwind but took a lot of water through the hole in the bow on the downwind legs. *Australia IV* crossed the finishing line 24 seconds ahead but the jury later disqualified her under Rule 35 (limitations on altering course), finding that with both yachts on port tack, *Australia IV* about a boat length to windward and one third of a boat length ahead, *Kookaburra III* luffed head to wind and tacked in a continuous movement. *Australia IV* luffed as *Kookaburra III* luffed head to wind with her stern swinging to leeward. *Kookaburra III* completed her tack and the collision occurred between a point three feet from the stern on *Australia IV's* starboard quarter and *Kookaburra III's* bow. Had *Australia IV* not luffed, *Kookaburra III's* bow would have cleared *Australia IV's* stern.

That was the last day of scheduled racing, but Series D was not over with the Taskforce 87 syndicate applying to the jury to have the genniker protest re-opened. This infuriated Warren Jones, executive director of the Bond syndicate, who for some time had been attacking the number and nature of the technical protests lodged.

A total of 50 protests were lodged from the 101 defender races and the

'Yes we could do with a hand up here mate.' Foredeck cooperation on Australia IV.

hearings were usually lengthy affairs. Of the protests lodged, 17 were from *Kookaburra II*, 12 from *Australia IV* and eight from *Kookaburra III*. *Kookaburra II* won four protests, *Kookaburra II* three, *Australia IV* two. The reason for the length of the protest hearings and to a lesser degree their frequency was the closeness of the races and the great volume of technical evidence available from the yachts' onboard computers, video shot from tenders, chase boats and helicopters and on *Kookaburra II* from 'racecam', the onboard camera recording the crew work and the movements of the opposing yacht for the television audience.

Supporting Taskforce's request to re-open the genniker protest, Iain Murray claimed the jury had acted outside its jurisdiction and overruled the evidence of the measurers. If the matter was not resolved satisfactorily, it could be taken to Court.

Warren Jones dropped his famous remark about *Kookaburra II's* protest: 'They howl like dingoes when they get beaten.' Jones said the threat of legal action put the jury under 'incredible duress'.

After four and a half hours they agreed on a formula to stop the Australian defence effort foundering in the protest room. *Australia IV* and *Kookaburra III* would sail a best five of nine final series irrespective of the request to reopen the protest. *Kookaburra II* would undergo further development and would trial against the winner of the final to decide which yacht was faster. The winning finalist, could if they wished sail *Kookaburra II* in the America's Cup match.

The following day, when it no longer mattered, the jury denied *Kookaburra II's* request to re-open the protest, concluding that in view of the ambiguity of the 12-Metre rating rule as it pertained to balloon jibs, the manner adopted by *Australia IV* in setting and changing the sail was consistent with a reasonable interpretation of the rules applying at the time. The measurers later moved to close the loophole in the rule permitting the assymetrical spinnakers to be built under balloon jib measurements, set down measurement limits for luff and leech lengths and for the mid girth width and

Australia IV *flew the genniker tacked to the bow like a normal headsail while gybing after the measurement committee's new restrictions on the controversial sail.*

Overleaf: Foul up that cost Kookaburra II *a race headsail on the way up plaited with the spinnaker on the way down.*

Tight bow-to-bow evenness of the racing yachts contrasts sharply against the vastness of the Indian Ocean. Kookaburra III *and* Australia IV.

But the traffic on the race course was as busy as a city street. Australia IV's, *Colin Beashel anxiously checks the proximity of* Kookaburra II's *bow.*

Overleaf: Kookaburra II's *call for room to round the wing mark was ignored by* Australia IV *on day six of the semi-finals.* Kookaburra II *had to alter course sharply to avoid collision and won the subsequent protest.*

No joy on Australia IV, *defeated again by* Kookaburra III, *end of a long road in sight.*

Right: The sort of team really needed to run a 12-Metre. The Taskforce team on mass jumped aboard Kookaburra III *after their final win.*

Overleaf: Jubilation for the crew after Kookaburra III's *final triumph over* Australia IV *while Kevin Parry frames his smile for the ever present television cameras.*

specified the spinnaker pole should remain approximately on the centreline of the yacht when the genniker was flown.

The final opened with a crash in the pre-start manoeuvres of the first race. Peter Gilmour went on board *Kookaburra III* as starting helmsman and, during some ferocious circling, *Kookaburra III's* bow mounted *Australia IV's* transom. *Kookaburra III*, with an upwind speed edge in the 18-20 knot wind, beat *Australia IV* by 29 seconds. At 0345 the following day, after a second eight hour hearing, the jury announced it had disqualified both yachts: *Australia IV* for as port tack yacht failing to keep clear of *Kookaburra III* in a collision incident; *Kookaburra III* under Rule 36 (port and starboard) with the jury finding that *Australia IV* on right-of-way starboard tack had to bear away to avoid a collision with *Kookaburra III* on port.

The following day, with afterguard members of both yachts short of sleep from their night with the jury, the start was a sedate affair, going to *Australia IV* by two seconds. *Kookaburra III* with a very definite upwind speed edge in the 15/25 knot sou'wester won by a decisive 1:34 although her crew had an anxious last five minutes when the carriage supporting the headboard of the mainsail collapsed and hinged down, leaving the sail flapping inside out but still partially effective.

The finals were never as close as the semis with *Kookaburra III* gaining an upwind edge in the break between the series to dominate *Australia IV*. The addition of Gilmour as starting helmsman was a good move, taking a lot of the pressure off Murray. After losing the first start badly, he went for even starts until the last race when his lightning response to a last minute gybe by *Australia IV* put him in complete control and he was able to split her off on the committee boat to win the start by 36 seconds. *Kookaburra III's* winning margins were 1:34, 0:46, 2:06, 1:13, 0:55.

Smiles were rare for Iain Murray but meaningful when they came.

Challenger Semi-finals and Finals

The Louis Vuitton Cup final was between *New Zealand 7* and *Stars & Stripes* – that came as no real surprise, except perhaps in the margins by which the winners of the semi-finals defeated their opponents. *New Zealand 7* was expected to continue in her winning ways; she ended with a record of 37 wins from 38 starts; but *French Kiss* might have provided closer opposition. The real upset was in the failure of *USA* to produce the speed which she had threatened against a much improved *Stars & Stripes*.

The ease with which the Kiwis despatched *French Kiss* was almost indecent. There was only one race in which the French showed any fire and in that they were aided by a rare gear failure aboard the Kiwi's boat. The same was almost true for Conner and Blackaller; their series was extremely anticlimactic after the three races which they had had during the rounds robin.

Conner's trim was so close to the marks this time that on a remeasurement after a race he had to swap six wet spinnakers for six dry ones and some headsails as well to satisfy the measurers. Conner took big strides in his sail inventory. There was little chance to develop sails outside the 18/24 knot wind range while they sailed in Hawaii; an explanation of why *Stars & Stripes* performance in lighter winds had been suspect, to say the least.

What the French did was to change their very elegant Philippe Briand design into the ugliest 12-Metre of all time – 'We have cut 80 centimetres off our transom,' said Marc Pajot in a totally bland voice. The effect was nothing short of visually devastating.

The man with the fast tongue and the radical boat had almost run out of things to do to make his boat go faster, or, even, control it. Blackaller did have new sails for this round and had been able to test them. All he had done to the boat was to optimise the twin rudder configuration for rough water, but exactly how he did that, he kept to himself.

By finishing fourth in the rounds robin, *French Kiss* experienced the rough

Cut off in its prime, the stern of French Kiss *is uglier than sin. A remarkably un-aesthetic move to achieve more speed, which failed.*

Overleaf: Egyptian cotton went out before the war but the French insisted on pyramid design in their Kevlar sail for French Kiss. *The 'contour' stripe across the jib shows that the hooked leech still existed.*

end of the deal and had to meet the Kiwis (33 wins from 34 races) in the semi-final. On the other hand they dropped their bombshell as the 10 minute gun fired and hoisted a protest flag as they had predicted that they would. It was a protest against the glassfibre construction of *New Zealand 7*, which was dismissed. The French had earlier intimated that they would go to the *New York State Supreme Court, which they considered to be the legal arbiter in matters concerning the Cup, to settle the legality of the glassfibre 12-Metre but withdrew that, happily for all concerned.

In the first race there was some of the tightest match race duelling of the summer when the two boats threw in 22 tacks each and two false tacks in the first mile but by then *New Zealand 7* was ahead and after rounding the first mark with a 61 second lead, there was never any doubt that the Kiwis would win the race; she did so by 2:46.

In the second race, from an even start the Kiwis rounded the first mark 42 seconds ahead, a repeat of the previous day with a winning margin of 2:40. The next race was more of a contest. *French Kiss* was only 22 seconds behind at the first mark with the wind at around 20 knots and closed to 14 seconds at the leeward mark. It was there that the Kiwi crew were flatfooted for a moment when the spinnaker pole end failed to open so that they could gather in the spinnaker. The French seized on the opportunity and went ahead, staying there until 300 yards from the line when after being slam dunked, *New Zealand 7* luffed and caught *French Kiss* unaware. After losing by 13 seconds, *French Kiss* was disqualified after protest.

The French won the start of the last race, pinning the Kiwis up against the committee boat but the speed of the *New Zealand 7* took her out to a lead which increased on most legs and she finished 2:44 ahead to take the semi-final with a 4-0 scoreline.

Tom Blackaller started this semi-final series knowing that he had won twice against Dennis Conner and had led for most of the other race. Despite that, and subsequently saying that *USA* had never gone faster, he was to lose in four

---

*The New York State Supreme Court would, if requested, have an interest only in matters concerning the Deed of Gift and not in those matters which relate to the 12-Metre rule or Lloyds scantlings.

*Very occasionly the ugliest duckling (*French Kiss) *could lead the elegant swan (*New Zealand 7).*

straight races. Blackaller led around all seven marks of the course in the first race only to lose on the last beat as the wind increased to 18 knots and *Stars & Stripes* seemed more in control. There was but 10 seconds between them on the line. In subsequent races it was all Conner, winning by margins of 3:02, 2:23 and 0.43 for a 4-0 scoreline.

When it came to the final it was Conner the mean; Conner the moody; Conner the magnificent; Conner back to the Conner of 1980, winning much as he pleased. The determined approach, the masterly execution and the years of experience were all there in profusion and as a driving force, the burning desire to recover the Cup for America, made Conner the man in control. It was the 'best 12-Metre match racer in the world', in his element.

Chris Dickson had to admit, when it was all over, 'I guess 13 years' experience beat 13 months' experience.' He was oh so right. *Stars & Stripes* was like an extension of Conner's arms and legs and his only defeat came as the result of a gear failure in a series which was held in the brisk breezes associated with the Fremantle Doctor on duty. Even when things went wrong, Conner was phlegmatic, knowing that his crew would put them right faster than any other. They were a highly trained unit, many of whom had sailed with Dennis in previous 12-Metre campaigns.

The Kiwis, in contrast, failed under pressure. They had a 37 win, one loss scoreline going into this series and were somewhat fortunate to win the one race which they did. They had a fraction less boat speed but showed that when they were ahead they could keep *Stars & Stripes* behind. They were beaten mainly because Dennis Conner wouldn't let them play the game their way. *New Zealand 7* was marginally faster tacking and in coming out of the tacks but while Conner could straight line it, he held sway. The tacking duels of the third race proved how vulnerable the Californian would be to this type of racing, but the Kiwis could never set him up for more. They lost with grace but, one suspects, with a certain amount of bewilderment.

In the first race Conner split with 30 seconds to go to the start and the Kiwis

Stars & Stripes *evaluating sails.*

'Everything produced in my company is perfect,' said Alberto Calderon, the designer of USA. *Skipper Tom Blackaller and 10 million aesthetes would argue otherwise.*

Calderon or Blackaller...you pays your money, you takes your choice...and here's your evidence.

tacked to parallel him as the gun fired, but Conner was up and away. When he tacked, he was ahead, held the lead on the run and doubled it to 30 seconds on the second beat. On the two reaches *New Zealand 7* made up time but by the end of the third beat Conner had the race under control with a lead of 41 seconds. He was able to pull away on the run and add another half minute on the final beat. The Kiwis suffered their second defeat of the summer and all those wins in the early series now meant nothing.

The second race saw *Stars & Stripes* 38 seconds up at the first mark and on the run the Kiwis struck back, knocking 20 seconds off the Californian's lead. Dickson had climbed on to *Stars & Stripes'* air and done it successfully, but that was to be his only success. Conner, setting a Mylar balloon jib, even went away on one of the reaches and was very much faster upwind.

Dickson afterwards admitted that he had lacked speed. 'We're looking for another gear,' he said, 'Once in front, Dennis didn't make any mistakes and you need speed to beat that.' The Kiwis called a lay day to try to find that speed.

It was in this race that records were broken; one record that the grinders on both boats could have done without and another which must have put heart into the New Zealanders. The world's longest letter of support, with more than 200,000 signatories, arrived as part of the pre-race hype at the Kiwis' dock. With it were New Zealand dignitaries and a group of Maori warriors in warpaint to perform the ceremonial Haka in front of more than 6,000 New Zealand supporters. Overhead an aeroplane towed a banner which proclaimed, 'If anyone can, a Kiwi can.' From a country where the support is definitely national, the evidence was plain to see.

Conner led around the windward mark by 21 seconds and a gybe set protected the inside overlap; the kite which was hoisted was one which came from the wardrobe of *America II.* The plan seemed perfect but as the spinnaker went up on *New Zealand 7,* the one on *Stars & Stripes* fell into the sea. As it went overboard so too did the genoa and the foredeck of *Stars & Stripes* was like a battlefield with crewmen struggling to get the sails back on board and

The New Zealanders had tremendous support from their countrymen in their final against Stars & Stripes, *but even a Maori war party could not sink Conner's hopes.*

Overleaf: Nobody ever said that racing a 12-Metre was a pleasurable occupation in the rough waters of Gage Roads.

the spinnaker rehoisted on another halyard. The snap shackle had sprung to release the sail. By the time it was up again the Kiwis were right on the Americans' stern. Dickson harried all the way down the run and managed to claim the inside overlap.

Conner instigated a tacking duel on the next beat and both boats went about 35 times. On the third beat, with the boats just 19 seconds apart at the start, there were 29 tacks but it was on the final leg to windward that records toppled.

Gretel and *Weatherly* did 58 tacks on a six mile beat in 1962; and on the final leg of the 1983 Cup series Conner made Bertrand cover him 47 times on a four and a half mile beat; but in this race Conner and the Kiwis tacked 55 times in 3¼ miles, once every 40 seconds! The Kiwis' winning margin was 0:38.

After the previous race, the next was anticlimactic. At the start, Conner, at the pin on starboard, was ahead and tacked to parallel the Kiwis. *Stars & Stripes* was simply higher and faster and 23 seconds ahead at the first mark.

Dickson compounded the deficit at the end of the run with an all standing gybe that took out the backstay and a couple of the aerials off the stern. Conner powered away and problems came *New Zealand 7's* way when the luff zipper on the mainsail gave trouble and finally the sail blew to pieces as she crossed the finishing line. But Conner was more than the master of the day; he had set himself up for the kill.

The fifth race was delayed for 45 minutes when the pin end buoy on the starting line moved. The pre-start was decidedly non-combative; neither boat moved into the area until there were three and a half minutes to go. Dennis pushed the Kiwis towards the pin end of the line, seemingly 'leaning' on them and forcing them to leeward so that they could be in danger of being outside the starboard tack lay line to the pin. At 30 seconds to go, he put in a short tack and with 15 seconds to the gun, Conner tacked on to starboard to parallel *New Zealand 7,* which did have a slight problem in getting inside the mark. The

'I'd go a million miles for one of those smiles Ma – aa – mmy'.

Erle Williams poised on the foredeck on New Zealand 7 *as she comes into the mark in pursuit of* Stars & Stripes.

Conner keeping Dickson at bay as they go into the gybe mark.

Overleaf: 'Hi folks, I did it again.' Conner waves while the crew smiles.

bow of *Stars & Stripes* went down momentarily to gain speed, came up, and the drag race was on.

The Kiwis tacked and dipped Conner's stern. The Californian slam dunked them perfectly. The Kiwis pulled off to leeward to make enough room to tack and when they did Conner went with them again, but loosely and the drag race was on with a vengeance.

At the weather mark *Stars & Stripes* gybe set while the Kiwis, rounding 42 seconds later, went for a bear away set. Conner had up a huge spinnaker but the lighter displacement of *New Zealand 7* was a telling factor. She surged up to be only 23 seconds down at the leeward mark. Then Dennis started to draw away again on the next beat but half a mile from the weather mark his number six genoa blew to pieces.

It was then that the months of training in the big breezes off Hawaii showed through. Within two minutes the number seven genoa was on deck, the burst sail cleared and the new jib hoisted. All the time Conner coolly steered the boat to windward under mainsail alone. Thirteen years of 12-Metre sailing experience was brought into play. The Kiwis were right up to *Stars & Stripes* and, unbelievably, they failed to come over to him on starboard tack and make him dip while they slam dunked as the headsail was going up. Instead they allowed him to hoist unhindered and tacked to leeward. That gave Conner the chance to tack right on their wind on the short leg to the mark and the gap was 14 seconds as they set off down the first reach and the spinnaker was slow going up on *New Zealand 7*. When it did fly, it proved to be a balloon jib and it pulled with such effect that the gap at the gybe was only eight seconds. The next reach was less shy but, deliberately, Conner went high, knowing that when the two had to bear off for the mark his spinnaker would be more effective than the Mylar headsail which the Kiwis had set.

When the Kiwis came to the inevitable peel to a running kite, they were in all sorts of strife. They tripped away both sails and ended up running to the mark bearheaded and the gap stretched to 16 seconds. Conner added another

As the wind comes up prior to the start, a quick headsail change brings five men to the foredeck of Stars & Stripes.

...From which position, there is little that New Zealand 7 *can do...*

Crewmen sit oblivious of the space age 'riblets', the high tech plastic covering on the hull of Stars & Stripes.

Overleaf: An expensive reticulation aboard Stars & Stripes *as wine and spirits soared with the success of being selected as the challenger.*

20 seconds to that on the third beat but the Kiwis downwind speed almost gobbled that up. They approached the last mark just nine seconds down and then Chris Dickson made his only mistake of his Cup summer in Fremantle; he hit the buoy. The re-rounding took 30 seconds but it took *New Zealand 7* out of the running and the fire went out of the Kiwis.

CHAPTER FIVE

The America's Cup Final

The America's Cup Final

The 26th Defence of the America's Cup failed; only the second one to do so and the Cup left Australia after so few heady, memorable days, just like the five days and four races that it took Dennis Conner to enter the yachting history books as the first man to win the Cup back after first losing it.

In the four races Murray never really got a look in. Conner had the faster boat and the greater class. The technology which had gone into *Stars & Stripes* was immense and the collecting and coordinating of it a precise and orderly operation. Much praise is therefore due to John Marshall, the design co-ordinator for the Sail America Foundation, who combined the talents of Britton Chance, Bruce Nelson and David Pedrick and fed them with the technology from the various scientific organisations which became involved with the *Stars & Stripes* campaign.

Not only was his boat faster but Conner also displayed the true match racer's talents. His 10,000 hours of 12-Metre sailing experience were evident as *Stars & Stripes* became an extension of his arms and legs. He placed the boat exactly where he wanted to and was able to lure Murray into presenting himself for the kill. Conner knew, from experience, whether or not *Kookaburra III* was up to full speed and when therefore to force Murray into making a tack which would result in him losing further ground.

Conner planned his campaign to peak at the first race of the America's Cup and he was helped by the opportunity to cull through the sails of the other American syndicates. He chose two of his arch-rival Tom Blackaller's mainsails and some of the light air spinnakers from *America II*, and these were in evidence during the racing. In addition, he used the days between the challenger trials and the grand final to test sails and to improve his crew's techniques. He wasted no time at all and after the first leg of the first race, Conner was never under pressure. Murray was just not able to take the game to him and seemingly gave up. Conner, by applying experience and talent,

Chairman of the Royal Perth Yacht Club's America's Cup committee, Dr. Stan Reid, signalling the opening of the America's Cup match in a ceremony at the club's Fremantle annexe.
Previous page: Here we go round the mulberry bush. Kookaburra III *chasing* Stars & Stripes *through spectator fleet, start of race four.*

The whole of Australia swung behind Kookaburra III *in the Cup match; it didn't happen until then.*

Gilmour, towing out to the first race: 'How do you feel we are going to go?' Murray:
'We are in good shape, we are going to do it.'

controlled the racing. He was brilliantly served by tactician Tom Whidden and navigator Peter Isler, and by a crew many of whom have been with him since 1980 and some since 1974.

The Racing

Race 1. Wind 225° 10/12 knots wind 165° 6/8 knots wind 205° 16/18 190 wind 10 knots

A grey and overcast day more reminiscent of Newport, Rhode Island than Fremantle may well have made Dennis Conner a happy man; by the end of it he certainly was. The conditions caused a 20 minute delay to the start, while the wind made some attempt to settle, but it was going to be one of those days in which it never did decide from whence it should blow; the windward mark was changed on each of the four beats.

With six minutes to go to the start, the two boats emerged from the spectator fleet and what followed was strange for the two yachts involved in an America's Cup final, at least if the pre-publicity was to be believed! The two yachts circled once; then they made towards the starting line with *Kookaburra III* coming astern of *Stars & Stripes*. With two and a half minutes to go Conner slowed the boat and brought *Kookaburra III* up to his starboard side. In doing so he effectively refused Gilmour access to the pin end of a four hundred yard start line and, there and then, he dictated the strategy of the start. The two boats sailed parallel for another minute and a quarter until Conner luffed; to gain height and to slow the boat. Gilmour answered and when Conner bore off gently, Gilmour bore away hard to try to go under *Stars & Stripes'* stern, but he had no way on and Conner was able to go across his bow and gain the lee side again. With 45 seconds to the start, Gilmour tacked away after Conner had luffed him to break the line. This meant, in the 8/10 knot breeze, that he would tack twice before starting as he couldn't scoop down and make the Committee Boat because he had too much time to go, and that would leave

The America's Cup buoy, a mark of the starting line and also the leeward mark. Kookaburra III *leaves her spinnaker drop to the last minute.*

All hell let loose. Peel from spinnaker to genniker.

The second reach became very shy when the wind veered. Stars & Stripes *is going for a genniker one third of the way down the leg while Don McCracken cleans the halyards up* Kookaburra III's *mast in order that she can do the same.*

him with less way on as he crossed the line.

Conner chose the pin end because the wind had backed some 15 degrees and favoured it. As Gilmour tacked away, Conner was able to put the bow of his boat down into a reach and aim for the buoy, a start timed to perfection. The line bias had given him almost a couple of boat lengths' lead as the gun fired and there was another coming as he was travelling a full knot faster.

After one minute, Conner put down the wheel and tacked towards *Kookaburra III* where Iain Murray was now behind the wheel. Murray, on starboard, realised that he wasn't going to cross or put Conner about so he tacked to leeward in the hope that the wind would veer. It didn't and Murray was caught on the outside of a further backing of the wind as the two drag raced to the right hand corner of the course.

After a few minutes, Peter Isler, the navigator of *Stars & Stripes,* appeared on the weather side with a long stick. He reached over the side of the boat with it to clear weed which had become attached to the rudder.

As *Stars & Stripes* went round the first mark, up went one of *America II's* spinnakers, to join the mainsail borrowed from Tom Blackaller's *USA;* and because of the backing wind, the run had become a reach with spinnaker poles on the headstay. An increase in wind halfway down the leg necessitated spinnaker peels by both boats; Conner going for another from US 46. Conner began the second beat with a classic piece of strategy. After rounding the leeward mark, he went for half the distance of his lead, tacked and, as Murray rounded, tacked again. It put him dead to windward of his opponent.

Murray halved the time difference on the second beat but it was to be his only significant gain of the day. The wind had shifted again and turned the first reach into a very broad one, Murray gybing twice on the leg. Spinnakers were handed for gennikers at the gybe mark and a third of the way down the leg they too were replaced by genoas as the wind continued to veer. From then on the race was very processional.

Result: *Stars & Stripes* bt *Kookaburra III* 1:41 1-0

Part of Stars & Stripes' *new found downwind speed came from spinnakers handed on from* America II.

A delighted Dennis Conner is congratulated by syndicate head Malin Burnham.

Support from the ladies of the upper echelon for the Stars & Stripes.

Race 2. Wind 195° 22/26 knots

Conner protected the left hand side of the starting line but with three minutes to go Gilmour slipped under *Stars & Stripes'* stern. As he came level Conner went into a slow tack and when Gilmour went to cover, the speed of *Kookaburra III*, as she went on to port tack, carried her again level with the American boat. At this time they were close to the line and about five lengths from the Committee Boat.

With 50 seconds to go to the start, Conner luffed and put Gilmour the wrong side of the line. As soon as Gilmour committed himself to going around the Committee Boat, Conner did a smart gybe and lined himself up to go flat out for the line. Gilmour's forced approach was a hurried one with a crash gybe around the stern of the boat; he was credited with winning the start, by three seconds, but Conner was ahead within a minute because he was going faster when the gun fired.

What followed was a starboard tack drag race for 14 minutes, until the two boats were two minutes from the lay line. Then, with a slight header experienced by both boats, *Kookaburra III* tacked away. Murray could see that he could be trapped beyond the starboard tack lay line if he allowed Conner to tack first. *Stars & Stripes* rounded 12 seconds ahead.

As they ran off Murray tried to blanket *Stars & Stripes* but Conner cleverly kept out of his wind shadow and began to pull away slightly; enough, it happened, to be able to gybe away, leaving the inside overlap unprotected, to go for a well judged line to the leeward mark.

On the second beat Conner put the issue beyond doubt, powering away to a minute and a quarter lead. It was the way he sailed the boat through the waves that probably gained him the extra distance. He chooses his path through the waves so that he can put his bow down to gain speed and then lift up to windward over the crest of a wave with real speed on. It looks to be a drunken reeling path, as though he keeps losing control, but it is devilishly effective.

Dressing for another wet day on Gage Roads.

Typically Stars & Stripes *led* Kookaburra III *from a deep approach to the starting line, alternately stalling and sailing.*

The first windward mark and only 12 seconds between them.

Overleaf: Chase boat cheers and checks Stars & Stripes *after her victory in windy race two.*

Left: At the end of the second run Stars & Stripes *dropped her spinnaker a long way from the mark, a very conservative approach by Dennis Conner...*

...but it did enable him to have the boat cleared away so that he could tack when ever he wanted to cover Kookaburra III....

Overleaf left: 'Don't we deserve to be happy, we're two nil up.'
Overleaf right: 'And we're two nil down.'

Conner became conservative. He hoisted a spinnaker he knew and trusted and set off down the reach while Murray put up one of *Australia IV's* gennikers, nicknamed 'The Thing' because it always brought her back to life, and then one of the same boat's staysails underneath it. Conner gained eight seconds. *Stars & Stripes* made a minor gain on the third beat and lost it on the run when Dennis went ultra-conservative in dropping his spinnaker early.

Result: *Stars & Stripes* bt *Kookaburra III* 1:10 2-0

Race 3. Wind 210° 12/18 knots

It seemed that each had settled early for which end of the line they wanted and so aggression was again dimmed; Conner wanted the pin and Murray the boat end. They started as they chose, on opposite tacks, and the advantage was with *Kookaburra III* as the wind had swung into the west slightly.

Enough it seemed to have Conner tack after a minute and harry Murray while bowman Donny McCracken was up the mast. He was up there for three tacks, trying to sort out the luff zipper on the mainsail and then came a short drag race out to the left hand side of the course. Fourteen minutes into the race Conner began a short tacking duel. Three times he went into a lee bow position, each time gaining a short amount and then, on the fourth occasion, Conner pulled away boldly to dip the stern of *Kookaburra III* when he saw that she was not up to full speed. When Murray went to slam dunk he lost out as Conner was able to sail through the lee of *Kookaburra III*. It was the turning point in the race; Conner was on the right hand side and from then on each time he went towards Murray he had right of way. *Stars & Stripes* rounded the first mark 15 seconds up.

Conner then took advantage of the shift on the left hand side of the course. He did a bear away set and sailed into it and out of the disturbed air from the spectator boat fleet; Murray gybe set and went deep into the disturbed air zone. It was as though Conner had learned his lesson from the beginning of the fifth leg of the last race in Newport three and a half years ago, an opportunity Murray

Kookaburra III *leaving her gybe to the last possible moment.*

A familiar course for the summer, displayed by the Committee Boat Trinity, *210 degrees.*

'*Smoke that halyard.*' Stars & Stripes *crew work was immaculate throughout the Cup match.*

Overleaf: The highly curved sheer line of Stars & Stripes *saw her dubbed the 'Big Blue Banana'.*

hadn't had. *Kookaburra III* went into a flat patch and *Stars & Stripes* gained another half minute, putting the race almost beyond doubt.

Just after rounding the leeward mark, drama hit the race. The *Kookaburra III* chase boat went up alongside and, after some considerable consultation with the Race Committee, informed the crew that there had been a threat that a bomb had been placed aboard the boat. Kookaburra security had always been good and the threat was dismissed. Murray said afterwards that when the chase boat had come alongside with the information, 'We checked our option list and our immediate response was: "What's the bad news?" Then we thought maybe this is our chance to find out what life's all about after 12-Metre racing. We took the option to continue in the race because we were well behind; if the bomb went off it wasn't going to affect the result of the race.'

Result: *Stars & Stripes* bt *Kookaburra III* 1:46 3-0

Race 4. Wind 220°/210° 16/20 knots

From early on Conner made it clear to Gilmour that he was protecting the left hand end of the line. With a minute to go both yachts were stalled, almost head to wind, three lengths short of the line, and about four lengths from the buoy. Conner held there until there were 20 seconds to go and then bore off for speed and hit the line with the gun. Gilmour followed him, but by taking the initiative Conner had the advantage, crossing the line five seconds ahead and Gilmour was forced to tack as he handed the wheel to Iain Murray.

There was a short flurry of three tacks each and after five minutes Conner headed for the right hand side of the course into the building sea breeze. The next 'cross' came at nine minutes into the beat and Conner went to the left, ignoring Murray and sailing on the wind shifts. Then he came back, again to protect the right hand side but working to the left of the rhumb line as there is always a shift in the last mile to the mark on that side. At the mark it was *Stars & Stripes* by 26 seconds and both boats did bear away sets (Murray learning from his third race mistake).

Kookaburra III's *army of young supporters did not forsake their heroes in defeat.*

Peter Gilmour, Kookaburra III's *starting helmsman, worried Conner all the way to the starting line in race four. He alternately placed* Kookaburra III *to windward of* Stars & Stripes' *stern...*

...and then to leeward.

Conner on line for another clean mark rounding while Murray stares at the gap he knows he can't bridge in race four.

Right: Problem for Kookaburra III *as the spinnaker sheet flies free after the gybe around the wing mark.*

In defeat there was still grace from Murray and his crew.

The traditional three cheers from the Royal Perth YC.

Overleaf: The triumphant return. Stars & Stripes, *winner of the America's Cup, returns to Fremantle's Fishing Boat Harbour.*

Losers can please themselves.

Winners can cheer.

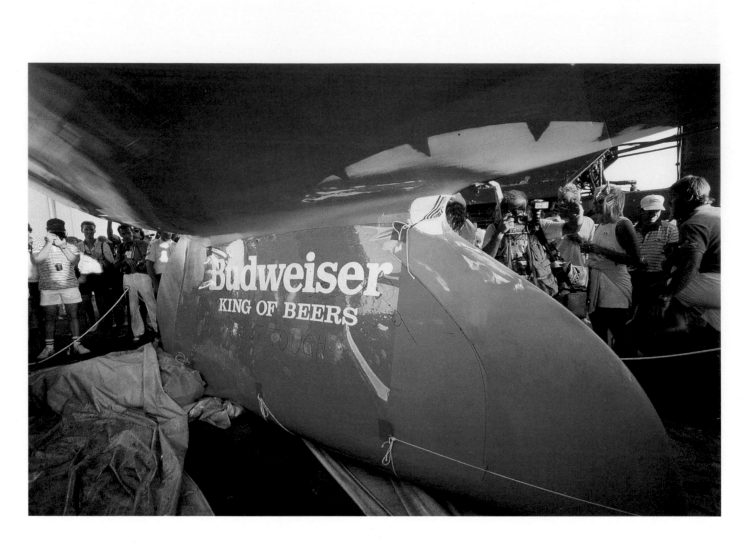

Everyone was surprised at the size of Stars & Stripes' *proboscis keel.*

Right: Dampen down Old Glory. Dock side celebrations begin.

Kookaburra III caught up marginally on the run but by the crucial second mark of the course *Stars & Stripes* was still ahead, a lead Conner increased to 42 seconds on the next beat. The reaches were unexciting, and it is probably the right time to observe that the America's Cup is the only major match racing event in which there are reaches in the course, although the gunsmoke blue boat did go a few more seconds ahead and on the next beat, with only a few tacks from either boat, *Stars & Stripes* was one tenth of a knot faster than *Kookaburra III* and started the final run 1:11 ahead. By the end it was 1:59 after a long drag race out to the right hand side of the course with Murray trailing Conner in a hopeless cause.
Result: *Stars & Stripes* bt *Kookaburra III* 1:59 4-0

Salute for the Anthems at the presentation: Royal Perth Yacht Club; 6th February, 1987.

Overleaf: A winner's smile reflected once more in the America's Cup.

APPENDIX

AMERICA'S CUP DEFENCE 1987 LIMITED
Club: Royal Perth YC
Syndicate head: Alan Bond

Boat: *Australia III*
Sail number: KA9
Designer: Ben Lexcen
Skipper: Gordon Lucas
Tactician: Carl Ryves

Boat: *Australia IV*
Sail number: KA 16
Designer: Ben Lexcen
Skipper: Colin Beashel
Tactician: Hugh Treharne

EASTERN AUSTRALIAN DEFENCE SYNDICATE
Club: Royal Perth YC
Syndicate head: Syd Fischer

Boat: *Steak 'n' Kidney*
Sail number: KA 14
Designer: Peter Cole
Skipper: Fred Neill/Phil Thompson
Tactician: Bernie Case

SOUTH AUSTRALIA CHALLENGE
Club: Royal Perth YC
Syndicate head: Sir James Hardy

Boat: *South Australia*
Sail number: KA 8
Designer: Ben Lexcen
Skipper: John Savage
Helmsman: Phil Thompson

TASKFORCE '87 LIMITED
Club: Royal Perth YC
Syndicate head: Kevin Parry

Boat: *Kookaburra II*
Sail number: KA 12
Designers: Iain Murray and
　　　　　John Swarbrick
Skipper: Peter Gilmour
Tactician: Andrew York

Boat: *Kookaburra III*
Sail number: KA 15
Designers: Iain Murray and
　　　　　John Swarbrick
Skipper: Iain Murray
Tactician: Derek Clark

HEART OF AMERICA CHALLENGE
Club: Chicago YC
Executive director: Alan Johnston

Boat: *Heart of America*
Sail number: US 51
Designers: Scott Graham and
　　　　　Eric Schlageter, Jim Gretsky
　　　　　(coordinator)
Skipper: Buddy Melges
Tactician: Dave Dellenbaugh

US MERCHANT MARINE ACADEMY FOUNDATION
Club: New York YC
Syndicate head: Richard de Vos

Boat: *America II*
Sail number: US 46
Designer: Sparkman & Stephens Inc.
　　　　　(Bill Langan)
Skipper: John Kolius
Tactician: John Bertrand

EAGLE FOUNDATION
Club: Newport Harbor YC
Syndicate head: Gary F Thomson

Boat: *Eagle*
Sail number: US 60
Designer: Johan Valentijn
Skipper: Rod Davis
Tactician: Doug Rastello

NEW ZEALAND CHALLENGE
Club: Royal New Zealand Yacht
　　Squadron
Syndicate head: Michael Fay

Boat: *New Zealand*
Sail number: KZ 7
Designers: Laurie Davidson, Bruce Farr
　　　　　and Ron Holland
Skipper: Chris Dickson
Tactician: Brad Butterworth

BRITISH AMERICA'S CUP CHALLENGE PLC
Club: Royal Thames YC
Syndicate head: Graham Walker

Boat: *White Crusader*
Sail number: K 24
Designers: Ian Howlett and
　　　　　David Hollom plus
　　　　　Herbert Pearcy and
　　　　　Stephen Wallis
Skipper: Harold Cudmore
Tactician: Chris Law

GOLDEN GATE FOUNDATION
Club: St Francis YC
Syndicate head: Ron Young

Boat: *USA*
Sail number: US 61
Designers: Gary Mull and
　　　　　Alberto Calderon
Skipper: Tom Blackaller
Tactician: Paul Cayard

Opposite page: One last reflection of the Royal Perth YC before the Cup is handed over.

SECRET COVE/TRUE NORTH
Club: Secret Cove YC in association with
    Royal Nova Scotia YS
Syndicate head: Paul Phelan

Boat: *Canada II*
Sail number: KC 2
Designer: Bruce Kirby
Skipper: Terry Neilson
Tactician: Greg Tawaststjerna

CHALLENGE KIS FRANCE
Club: Societe des Regattes Rochelaise
Syndicate head: Serge Crasnianski

Boat: *French Kiss*
Sail number: F 7
Designer: Philippe Briand
Skipper: Marc Pajot
Tactician: Marc Bouet

MARSEILLES SYNDICATE
Club: Societe Nautique de Marseilles
Syndicate head: M. Le Maire de
    Marseilles

Boat: *Challenge France*
Sail number: F 8
Designer: Daniel Andrieu
Skipper: Yves Pajot

AZZURRA SYNDICATE
Club: Yacht Club Costa Smeralda
Syndicate head: H.H. The Aga Khan

Boat: *Azzurra*
Sail number: I 10
Designer: Andrea Vallicelli, Sciomachen
Skipper: Mauro Pelaschier
Tactician: Tiziano Navo

SAIL AMERICA FOUNDATION
FOR INTERNATIONAL
UNDERSTANDING
Club: San Diego YC
Syndicate head: Malin Burnham

Boat: *Stars & Stripes*
Sail number: US 55
Designers: John Marshall (design

coordinator), Dave Pedrick,
    Britton Chance, Bruce Nelson
Skipper: Dennis Conner
Tactician: Tom Whidden

CONSORZIO ITALIA
Club: Yacht Club Italiano
Syndicate head: Admiral Angelo Monassi

Boat: *Italia*
Sail number: I 7
Designers: Giorgetti and Magrini
    (Ian Howlett, consultant)
Skipper: Aldo Migliaccio
Tactician: Tomasso Chieffi

COURAGEOUS CHALLENGE
Club: Yale Corinthian YC
Syndicate chairman: Leonard Greene

Boat: *Courageous IV*
Sail number: US 26
Designer: Roger Marshall and
    Leonard Greene
Skipper: David Vietor

DEFENDER RACES FOR THE AMERICA'S CUP

All times rounded up to the nearest second.

SERIES A

RACE DAY 1: 18 October 1986
Kookaburra II beat *Australia III* by 1 min 56 sec
Australia IV beat *South Australia* by 2 min 30 sec
Kookaburra III beat *Steak 'n' Kidney* by 4 min 3 sec

RACE DAY 2: 19 October 1986
Kookaburra III beat *Australia IV* by 43 sec
Kookaburra II beat *South Australia* by 4 min
Australia III beat *Steak 'n' Kidney* by 1 min 11 sec

RACE DAY 3: 20 October 1986
South Australia beat *Steak 'n' Kidney* by 1 min 12 sec
Kookaburra III beat *Australia III* by 4 min 30 sec
Australia IV beat *Kookaburra II* by 20 sec

RACE DAY 4: 21 October 1986
Australia IV beat *Steak 'n' Kidney* by 9 min 1 sec
Kookaburra III beat *Kookaburra II* by 2 sec
Australia III beat *South Australia* (retired)

RACE DAY 5: 22 October 1986
Kookaburra II beat *Steak 'n' Kidney* by 4 min 11 sec
Australia IV beat *Australia III* by 3 min 7 sec
Kookaburra III beat *South Australia* by 6 min 43 sec

RACE DAY 6: 24 October 1986
Kookaburra II beat *South Australia* by 3 min 16 sec
Australia IV beat *Kookaburra III* by 36 sec
Australia III beat *Steak 'n' Kidney* by 1 min 47 sec

RACE DAY 7: 25 October 1986
Kookaburra III beat *Australia III* by 1 min 58 sec

South Australia beat *Steak 'n' Kidney* by 2 min 16 sec
Kookaburra II beat *Australia IV* by 1 min 17 sec

RACE DAY 8: 26 October 1986
Kookaburra III beat *Kookaburra II* by 6 sec
Australia III beat *South Australia* by 2 min 17 sec
Australia IV beat *Steak 'n' Kidney* (retired)

RACE DAY 9: 27 October 1986
Kookaburra II beat *Steak 'n' Kidney* by 2 min 33 sec
Kookaburra III beat *South Australia* by 6 min 5 sec
Australia IV beat *Australia III* by 2 min 17 sec

RACE DAY 10: 28 October 1986
Australia IV beat *South Australia* by 2 min 8 sec
Kookaburra III beat *Steak 'n' Kidney* (retired)
Kookaburra II beat *Australia III* by 2 min 9 sec

SERIES B

RACE DAY 1: 9 November 1986
Australia IV beat *South Australia* (retired)
Kookaburra III beat *Steak 'n' Kidney* by 4 min
Kookaburra II beat *Australia III* by 2 min 7 sec

RACE DAY 2: 10 November 1986
Australia IV beat *Australia III* by 5 sec
Kookaburra II beat *Steak 'n' Kidney* by 3 min 25 sec
Kookaburra III beat *South Australia* by 2 min 25 sec

RACE DAY 3: 11 November 1986
Kookaburra III beat *Kookaburra II* by 1 min 34 sec
South Australia beat *Australia III* by 2 min 27 sec
Australia IV beat *Steak 'n' Kidney* by 5 min 23 sec

RACE DAY 4: 12 November 1986
Australia III beat *Steak 'n' Kidney* by 5 min 30 sec
Kookaburra III beat *Australia IV* by 3 min 18 sec
Kookaburra II beat *South Australia* by 1 min 41 sec

RACE DAY 5: 13 November 1986
Kookaburra II beat *Australia IV* by 1 min 41 sec
South Australia beat *Steak 'n' Kidney* by 24 sec
Kookaburra III beat *Australia III* by 2 min 1 sec

RACE DAY 6: 15 November 1986
Steak 'n' Kidney versus *South Australia*
(both yachts disqualified)

Kookaburra III beat *Kookaburra II* by 4 sec
Australia IV beat *Australia III* by 1 min 10 sec

RACE DAY 7: 16 November 1986
Kookaburra II beat *Steak 'n' Kidney* by 2 min 54 sec
Australia III beat *South Australia* by 1 min 42 sec
Kookaburra III beat *Australia IV* (disqualified)

RACE DAY 8: 17 November 1986
Kookaburra III beat *Australia III* by 2 min 7 sec
Australia IV beat *Steak 'n' Kidney* by 3 min 20 sec
Kookaburra II beat *South Australia* by 4 min 10 sec

RACE DAY 9: 18 November 1986
Kookaburra III beat *South Australia* by 1 min 9 sec
Australia IV beat *Kookaburra II* by 15 sec
Australia III beat *Steak 'n' Kidney* by 1 min 13 sec

RACE DAY 10: 19 November 1986
South Australia beat *Australia IV* by 1 min 36 sec
Kookaburra II beat *Australia III* by 24 sec
Kookaburra III beat *Steak 'n' Kidney* by 3 min 18 sec

SERIES C

RACE DAY 1: 2 December 1986
Kookaburra III beat *Kookaburra II* by 32 sec
Steak 'n' Kidney beat *South Australia* by 5 min 54 sec

RACE DAY 2: 3 December 1986
Kookaburra II beat *South Australia* by 14 min 59 sec
Australia IV beat *Steak 'n' Kidney* by 2 min 46 sec

RACE DAY 3: 4 December 1986
Australia IV beat *Kookaburra III* by 50 sec
Kookaburra II beat *Steak 'n' Kidney* by 39 sec

RACE DAY 4: 5 December 1986
Kookaburra III beat *Steak 'n' Kidney* by 1 min 52 sec
Australia IV beat *South Australia* by 7 min 31 sec

RACE DAY 5: 6 December 1986
Australia IV beat *Kookaburra II* by 20 sec
Kookaburra III beat *South Australia* (retired)

RACE DAY 6: 7 December 1986
Kookaburra III beat *Kookaburra II* by 26 sec
Australia IV beat *Steak 'n' Kidney* by 2 min 26 sec

RACE DAY 7: 9 December 1986
Steak 'n' Kidney beat *Kookaburra II* by 2 min 8 sec
Kookaburra III beat *Australia IV* (retired)

RACE DAY 8: 10 December 1986
Kookaburra II beat *Australia IV* by 5 min 11 sec
Kookaburra III beat *Steak 'n' Kidney* by 26 sec

RACE DAY 9: 12 December 1986
Kookaburra II beat *Kookaburra III* by 36 sec
Australia IV beat *Steak 'n' Kidney* by 1 min 8 sec

RACE DAY 10: 13 December 1986
Australia IV beat *Kookaburra III* by 14 sec
Steak 'n' Kidney beat *Kookaburra II* by 4 sec

RACE DAY 11: 14 December 1986
Kookaburra III beat *Steak 'n' Kidney* by 2 min 54 sec
Australia IV beat *Kookaburra II* (disqualified)

SERIES D (SEMI-FINALS)

RACE DAY 1: 27 December 1986
Australia IV beat *Steak 'n' Kidney* by 19 min
Kookaburra II beat *Kookaburra III* by 12 sec

RACE DAY 2: 28 December 1986
Kookaburra II beat *Steak 'n' Kidney* by 41 sec
Australia IV beat *Kookaburra III* by 12 sec

RACE DAY 3: 29 December 1986
Kookaburra II beat *Australia IV* by 59 sec
Kookaburra III beat *Steak 'n' Kidney* by 2 min 6 sec

RACE DAY 4: 30 December 1986
Australia IV beat *Steak 'n' Kidney* by 14 sec
Kookaburra II beat *Kookaburra III* by 50 sec

RACE DAY 5: 2 January 1987
Kookaburra II beat *Steak 'n' Kidney* by 2 min 2 sec
Kookaburra III beat *Australia IV* by 17 sec

RACE DAY 6: 3 January 1987
Steak 'n' Kidney beat *Kookaburra III* by 39 sec
Australia IV beat *Kookaburra II* by 41 sec

RACE DAY 7: 4 January 1987
Kookaburra III beat *Kookaburra II* by 8 min 57 sec

RACE DAY 8: 6 January 1987
Australia IV beat *Kookaburra II* by 24 sec

RACE DAY 9: 7 January 1987
Australia IV beat *Kookaburra III* by 24 sec

FINALS

RACE DAY 1: 14 January 1987
Kookaburra III versus *Australia IV* (both yachts disqualified)

RACE DAY 2: 15 January 1987
Kookaburra III beat *Australia IV* by 1 min 34 sec

RACE DAY 3: 16 January 1987
Kookaburra III beat *Australia IV* by 46 sec

RACE DAY 4: 17 January 1987
Kookaburra III beat *Australia IV* by 2 min 6 sec

RACE DAY 5: 19 January 1987
Kookaburra III beat *Australia IV* by 1 min 13 sec

RACE DAY 6: 20 January 1987
Kookaburra III beat *Australia IV* by 55 sec

Kookaburra III won the right to defend the America's Cup.

CHALLENGER RACES FOR THE AMERICA'S CUP
LOUIS VUITTON CUP

All times rounded up to the nearest second.

ROUNDS ROBIN 1

RACE DAY 1: 5 October 1986
Eagle beat *Challenge France* by 9 min 21 sec
Stars & Stripes beat *Italia* by 5 min 49 sec
New Zealand beat *Heart of America* by 6 min 29 sec
French Kiss beat *Azzurra* by 3 min 9 sec
White Crusader beat *USA* by 11 sec
America II beat *Canada II* by 1 min 6 sec

RACE DAY 2: 6 October 1986
New Zealand beat *Italia* by 1 min 49 sec
French Kiss beat *Eagle* by 27 sec
Stars & Stripes beat *Azzurra* by 3 min 19 sec
USA beat *Courageous* by 8 min 4 sec
White Crusader beat *Canada II* by 1 min 18 sec
Heart of America beat *Challenge France* by 1 min 44 sec

RACE DAY 3: 7 October 1986
Stars & Stripes beat *Eagle* by 3 min
New Zealand beat *USA* by 1 min 42 sec
French Kiss beat *Courageous* (retired)
America II beat *White Crusader* by 1 min 27 sec
Canada II beat *Heart of America* by 2 min 36 sec
Italia beat *Azzurra* by 5 min 10 sec

RACE DAY 4: 8 October 1986
New Zealand beat *French Kiss* by 40 sec
Stars & Stripes beat *White Crusader* by 1 min 16 sec
America II beat *USA* by 1 min 34 sec
Canada II beat *Challenge France* by 5 min 15 sec
Heart of America beat *Azzurra* by 18 sec
Eagle beat *Courageous* by 10 min 45 sec

RACE DAY 5: 9 October 1986
Stars & Stripes beat *USA* by 6 sec
Canada II beat *French Kiss* by 1 min 42 sec
White Crusader beat *Challenge France* by 4 min 16 sec
Italia beat *Heart of America* by 4 min 3 sec
Azzurra beat *Courageous* by 3 min 53 sec
New Zealand beat *America II* by 1 min 5 sec

RACE DAY 6: 10 October 1986
White Crusader beat *French Kiss* by 1 min 28 sec
USA beat *Heart of America* by 3 min 39 sec
Italia beat *Canada II* by 1 min 7 sec
Eagle beat *Azzurra* by 2 min 3 sec
America II beat *Courageous* by 11 min 33 sec
Stars & Stripes beat *Challenge France* by 4 min 42 sec

RACE DAY 7: 13 October 1986
USA beat *Canada II* by 47 sec
White Crusader beat *Azzurra* by 4 min 22 sec
Eagle beat *Heart of America* by 1 min 35 sec
New Zealand beat *Courageous* by 8 min 25 sec
America II beat *Challenge France* (retired)
French Kiss beat *Italia* (disqualified)

RACE DAY 8: 13 October 1986
White Crusader beat *Heart of America* by 3 min 21 sec
Canada II beat *Courageous IV* by 3 min 53 sec
New Zealand beat *Azzurra* by 4 min 55 sec
America II beat *Stars & Stripes* by 33 sec
Italia beat *Challenge France* by 1 min 38 sec
USA beat *Eagle* by 2 min 24 sec

RACE DAY 9: 14 October 1986
Canada II beat *Azzurra* (retired)

America II beat *Heart of America* by 4 min 6 sec
Stars & Stripes beat *Courageous* (retired)
Challenge France beat *French Kiss* (disqualified)
Italia beat *Eagle* by 1 min 34 sec
New Zealand beat *White Crusader* by 4 min

RACE DAY 10: 15 October 1986
Heart of America beat *Courageous IV* (disqualified)
Challenge France beat *Azzurra* (retired)
America II beat *French Kiss* by 33 sec
USA beat *Italia* by 3 min 52 sec
New Zealand beat *Eagle* by 4 min 41 sec
Stars & Stripes beat *Canada II* by 2 min 19 sec

RACE DAY 11: 17 October 1986
America II beat *Azzurra* by 6 min 34 sec
Italia beat *Courageous IV* (retired)
USA beat *Challenge France* (retired)
White Crusader beat *Eagle* by 4 min 43 sec
Stars & Stripes beat *New Zealand* by 43 sec
French Kiss beat *Heart of America* by 3 min 40 sec

RACE DAY 12: 18 October 1986
Courageous IV beat *Challenge France* by 1 min 7 sec
America II beat *Eagle* by 1 min 35 sec
Italia beat *White Crusader* by 2 min 19 sec
New Zealand beat *Canada II* by 2 min 37 sec
Stars & Stripes beat *French Kiss* by 3 min 40 sec
USA beat *Azzurra* by 5 min 22 sec

RACE DAY 13: 19 October 1986
New Zealand beat *Challenge France* by 6 min 3 sec
Canada II beat *Eagle* by 1 min 37 sec
Stars & Stripes beat *Heart of America* by 3 min 7 sec

USA beat *French Kiss* by 1 min 18 sec
White Crusader beat *Courageous IV* by 7 min 32 sec
America II beat *Italia* by 3 min 24 sec

ROUNDS ROBIN 2

RACE DAY 1: 2 November 1986
New Zealand beat *Heart of America* by 13 min 6 sec
White Crusader beat *Azzurra* by 2 min 1 sec
Italia beat *Challenge France* by 8 min 43 sec
America II beat *Eagle* by 1 min 49 sec
USA beat *Stars & Stripes* by 39 sec
French Kiss beat *Canada II* by 2 min 15 sec

RACE DAY 2: 3 November 1986
Canada II beat *Azzurra* by 2 min 17 sec
Heart of America beat *Challenge France* by 37 sec
New Zealand beat *Stars & Stripes* by 58 sec
America II beat *French Kiss* by 53 sec
White Crusader beat *Italia* by 2 min 14 sec
Eagle beat *USA* by 3 min 22 sec

RACE DAY 3: 4 November 1986
Stars & Stripes beat *Challenge France* by 4 min 51 sec
White Crusader beat *Canada II* by 1 sec
America II beat *Azzurra* by 1 min 30 sec
French Kiss beat *USA* by 44 sec
Italia beat *Heart of America* by 50 sec
New Zealand beat *Eagle* by 3 min 42 sec

RACE DAY 4: 5 November 1986
America II beat *White Crusader* by 1 min
Stars & Stripes beat *Heart of America* by 4 min 50 sec
Eagle beat *Challenge France* (retired)
Italia beat *Canada II* by 37 sec
USA beat *Azzurra* by 3 min 58 sec
New Zealand beat *French Kiss* by 2 min 23 sec

RACE DAY 5: 6 November 1986
Eagle beat *Heart of America* (retired)
America II beat *Canada II* by 3 min 41 sec
USA beat *White Crusader* (retired)
New Zealand beat *Azzurra* by 5 min 19 sec
French Kiss beat *Challenge France* by 4 min 1 sec
Stars & Stripes beat *Italia* by 5 min 15 sec

RACE DAY 6: 7 November 1986
USA beat *Canada II* by 4 min 6 sec
Stars & Stripes beat *Eagle* by 6 min 29 sec
French Kiss beat *Heart of America* by 1 min 50 sec
Azzurra beat *Challenge France* by 2 min 13 sec
New Zealand beat *White Crusader* by 1 min 28 sec
America II beat *Italia* by 1 min 32 sec

RACE DAY 7: 9 November 1986
Italia beat *Eagle* by 1 min 29 sec
America II beat *USA* by 1 min 18 sec
New Zealand beat *Canada II* by 3 min 10 sec
Heart of America beat *Azzurra* by 1 min 41 sec
Stars & Stripes beat *French Kiss* by 2 min 34 sec
White Crusader beat *Challenge France* by 11 min 53 sec

RACE DAY 8: 10 November 1986
New Zealand beat *America II* by 12 min 32 sec
French Kiss beat *Eagle* by 1 min 13 sec
USA beat *Italia* by 3 min 58 sec
White Crusader beat *Heart of America* by 7 min 10 sec
Canada II beat *Challenge France* by 6 min 2 sec
Stars & Stripes beat *Azzurra* by 37 sec

RACE DAY 9: 11 November 1986
French Kiss beat *Italia* by 1 min 39 sec
New Zealand beat *USA* by 1 min 25 sec
America II beat *Challenge France* by 3 min 16 sec
White Crusader beat *Stars & Stripes* by 2 min 18 sec
Eagle beat *Azzurra* by 17 sec
Canada II beat *Heart of America* by 4 min 5 sec

RACE DAY 10: 12 November 1986
USA beat *Challenge France* by 8 min 4 sec
New Zealand beat *Italia* by 5 min 47 sec
French Kiss beat *Azzurra* by 4 min 12 sec
Canada II beat *Stars & Stripes* by 29 sec
America II beat *Heart of America* by 4 min 10 sec
White Crusader beat *Eagle* by 3 min 18 sec

RACE DAY 11: 13 November 1986
Azzurra beat *Italia* (retired)
New Zealand beat *Challenge France* by 9 min 27 sec
USA beat *Heart of America* by 2 min 29 sec
Canada II beat *Eagle* by 1 min 32 sec
French Kiss beat *White Crusader* by 4 min 25 sec
Stars & Stripes beat *America II* by 1 min 31 sec

ROUNDS ROBIN 3

RACE DAY 1: 2 December 1986
French Kiss beat *Azzurra* by 3 min 42 sec
New Zealand beat *Challenge France* by 7 min 29 sec
Italia beat *USA* by 12 min 39 sec
Stars & Stripes beat *Canada II* by 3 min 46 sec
White Crusader beat *Eagle* by 5 min 14 sec
Heart of America beat *America II* by 56 sec

RACE DAY 2: 3 December 1986
New Zealand beat *Heart of America* by 3 min 27 sec
Italia beat *Azzurra* by 14 min 41 sec
French Kiss beat *White Crusader* (retired)
Stars & Stripes beat *America II* by 13 min 4 sec
USA beat *Challenge France* by 11 min 29 sec
Canada II beat *Eagle* by 6 min 16 sec

RACE DAY 3: 4 December 1986
White Crusader beat *Italia* by 2 min 27 sec
Heart of America beat *Challenge France* by 8 min
New Zealand beat *Stars & Stripes* by 32 sec
America II beat *Eagle* by 8 min 36 sec
USA beat *Azzurra* by 3 min 30 sec
French Kiss beat *Canada II* by 4 min 21 sec

RACE DAY 4: 5 December 1986
Stars & Stripes beat *Challenge France* by 10 min 48 sec
White Crusader beat *Azzurra* by 3 min 57 sec
Canada II beat *Italia* (retired)
Heart of America beat *USA* by 36 sec
New Zealand beat *Eagle* by 6 min
French Kiss beat *America II* by 7 sec

RACE DAY 5: 7 December 1986
Canada II beat *Azzurra* by 3 min 50 sec
Stars & Stripes beat *Heart of America* by 1 min 32 sec
Eagle beat *Challenge France* by 3 min 5 sec
New Zealand beat *French Kiss* by 4 min 43 sec
America II beat *Italia* (retired)
USA beat *White Crusader* by 3 sec

RACE DAY 6: 8 December 1986
Heart of America beat *Eagle* by 3 min 57 sec
White Crusader beat *Canada II* by 3 min 55 sec
America II beat *Azzurra* by 1 min 49 sec
New Zealand beat *Italia* by 3 min 30 sec
French Kiss beat *Challenge France* (retired)
USA beat *Stars & Stripes* by 42 sec

RACE DAY 7: 9 December 1986
USA beat *Canada II* by 5 min 39 sec
Stars & Stripes beat *Eagle* by 10 min 11 sec
French Kiss beat *Heart of America* by 10 min 10 sec
New Zealand beat *Azzurra* by 6 min 8 sec
America II beat *White Crusader* by 1 min 47 sec
Italia beat *Challenge France* (retired)

RACE DAY 8: 12 December 1986
Stars & Stripes beat *French Kiss* by 2 min 7 sec
America II beat *Canada II* by 1 min 16 sec

USA beat *Eagle* by 5 min 51 sec
Azzurra beat *Challenge France* (retired)
Italia beat *Heart of America* by 22 sec
New Zealand beat *White Crusader* by 6 sec

RACE DAY 9: 13 December 1986
USA beat *America II* by 2 min 17 sec
French Kiss beat *Eagle* by 2 min 49 sec
Stars & Stripes beat *Italia* by 3 min 37 sec
White Crusader beat *Challenge France* (retired)
New Zealand beat *Canada II* by 2 min 54 sec
Heart of America beat *Azzurra* by 2 min 23 sec

RACE DAY 10: 14 December 1986
Italia beat *Eagle* by 36 sec
USA beat *French Kiss* by 1 min 51 sec
New Zealand beat *America II* by 15 sec
White Crusader beat *Heart of America* by 3 min 49 sec
Stars & Stripes beat *Azzurra* by 4 min 11 sec
Canada II beat *Challenge France* (retired)

RACE DAY 11: 15 December 1986
New Zealand beat *USA* by 59 sec
Italia beat *French Kiss* by 1 min 55 sec
Eagle beat *Azzurra* (retired)
Heart of America beat *Canada II* by 12 min 49 sec
America II beat *Challenge France* (retired)
Stars & Stripes beat *White Crusader* by 4 min 12 sec

SEMI-FINALS

RACE DAY 1: 28 December 1986
New Zealand beat *French Kiss* by 2 min 46 sec
Stars & Stripes beat *USA* by 10 sec

RACE DAY 2: 28 December 1986
Stars & Stripes beat *USA* by 3 min 2 sec
New Zealand beat *French Kiss* by 2 min 40 sec

RACE DAY 3: 30 December 1986
New Zealand beat *French Kiss* (disqualified)
Stars & Stripes beat *USA* by 2 min 23 sec

RACE DAY 4: 2 January 1987
Stars & Stripes beat *USA* by 43 sec
New Zealand beat *French Kiss* by 2 min 44 sec

FINALS

RACE DAY 1: 13 January 1987
Stars & Stripes beat *New Zealand* by 1 min 20 sec

RACE DAY 2: 14 January 1987
Stars & Stripes beat *New Zealand* by 1 min 36 sec

RACE DAY 3: 16 January 1987
New Zealand beat *Stars & Stripes* by 38 sec

RACE DAY 4: 17 January 1987
Stars & Stripes beat *New Zealand* by 3 min 38 sec

RACE DAY 5: 19 January 1987
Stars & Stripes beat *New Zealand* by 1 min 29 sec

AMERICA'S CUP MATCH

RACE DAY 1: 31 January 1987
Stars & Stripes beat *Kookaburra III* by 1 min 41 sec

RACE DAY 2: 1 February 1987
Stars & Stripes beat *Kookaburra III* by 1 min 10 sec

RACE DAY 3: 2 February 1987
Stars & Stripes beat *Kookaburra III* by 1 min 46 sec

RACE DAY 4: 4 February 1987
Stars & Stripes beat *Kookaburra III* by 1 min 59 sec